F1'89
Photo Review
ultimate all-color annual

Distributed by

Motorbooks International
Publishers & Wholesalers Inc ®

First published in 1990 by Motorbooks International
Publishers & Wholesalers, P O Box 2, 729 Prospect Avenue,
Osceola, WI 54020 USA

Produced by Vallardi & Associates (Milano), Italy

© Vallardi & Associates (Milano), 1989

ISBN 0-87938-375-5
Library of Congress Cataloguing in Publication Data

The publishing of this volume was made possible
through the kind collaboration of the
INA Istituto Nazionale delle Assicurazioni
and **ASSITALIA**
whose desire it was to offer the public
a photographic record of the very highest quality.
Text by: Andrea de Adamich and Oscar Orefici
Photographs by: Daniele Amaduzzi
Technical coordination: Giuseppe Malorni
Offset: Peca (Vaprio d'Adda), Fotolito 2000 (Bergamo) and TopColor (Milano)
Composition: Peca (Vaprio d'Adda)
Paper: Garda Art
Printing: CMT (Rodano - Milano)
Coordination: INA Press Office and Foreign Relations Office
Published by: Vallardi & Associates (Milano)
Printed in Italy

These Ferrari mechanics - the ultimate priests of a pagan speed ritual - very carefully prepare the cars for the race, working in silence and never complaining about the long hours. Tomes have been written about these Formula 1 mechanics, and while some of it a bit too rhetorical, every bit of it is necessary for properly understanding the colorful world of the speed circus.

McLaren

This team started out with all the forecasts in its favor, and this was no surprise to anyone because in 1988 it had racked up wins in 15 out of 16 Grand Prix world championship events. The turbos are out and the the non-turbos are in, but Honda was busy at work way before the competition got started. So, between the rumors, atmosphere and team manager Ron Dennis's confidence, it doesn't look like the competition is going to have much of a chance.

Then we have the team's two driving aces whose very similar experience, background, and ambition allow them to understand each other and work together perfectly.

So, this team looks like it's really still unbeatable. But, as is certainly well known in the world of F1, the favorites are always full of surprises, and each race seems to give the underdog special privileges. So, we really shouldn't "count our chickens before they're hatched". The McLaren certainly had to sweat out a lot of problems during this past season - one of its worst in recent years - what with the various polemics (almost riots at times) that forced Ron Dennis to make public some of the things he would have rather kept under cover. Then

is worth keeping in mind for the future, and that 1990 promises to be a particularly critical year in this respect because a non-turbocharged engine can only be improved so much. Furthermore, those that started out at a maximum level - as did the McLaren - will have less room for improvement than the others. Therefore, there are a number of cars with theoretically about the same performance, competitiveness and reliability.

Ron Dennis was firmly set on replacing Prost with Berger and this move should calm the waters a bit at the McLaren stable, Aryton Senna permitting.

The Drivers

Prost and Senna have now been together at McLaren for two seasons: 1988 and 1989. Senna scored brilliantly with his speed and skill, while Prost carefully applied his mature judgment, experience and racing strategy to correctly evaluate the risks required to come out the No.1 driver.

What appeared quite clear, however, was that you can never hope to keep two roosters in the

formance. Senna already had personal problems, some of them even psychological, and this combination of mental conditions were definitely at the bottom of Senna's slipping performance. It wasn't affecting his time trials as much as it was the consistency of his racing performance.

Senna's been too much in the habit of giving, and this is something that just won't do anymore. The team should have known better than to let the rivalry build up until it even got physical. For a winning Formula 1 team this was not only unbelievable but completely uncalled for. So now Prost can concentrate his thoughts on the Ferrari and Mansell, and look forward to proudly showing all of them over there what he can do.

Senna will keep on with McLaren, feeling a bit humiliated, perhaps even frustrated, and with the McLaren people a bit irked with him for having caused them to lose the No.1 driver to Ferrari.Berger might take advantage of this.

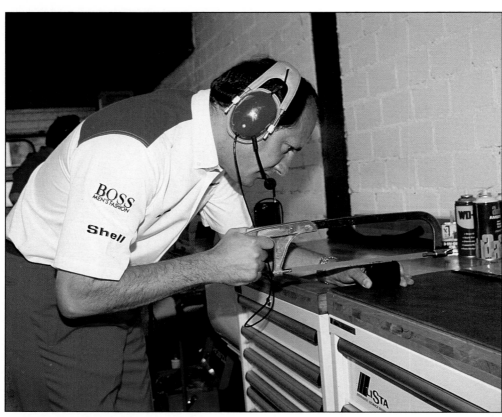

Alain Prost, figuring he was having to play second fiddle to Ayrton Senna (at least from the technical standpoint), said he'd had enough and went over to Ferrari. Prost's objections, however, were actually in contrast with the results he obtained, nothwithstanding the anguish of this difficult season.

McLaren's automotive engineering, including the engine, was advanced to the point of being able to keep its most aggressive adversaries at a safe distance.

As a matter of fact, the Ferrari proved that this

same coop unless they're both willing to make some concessions.

Senna seemed to have matured considerably, even more so that had Prost; with Senna's three wins in the first four races, the handwriting on the wall was very legible.

Ron Dennis and Honda naturally started to fawn a bit over Senna and this show of favoritism got Prost's goat. He turned bitter and kept continually complaining about this preferential treatment, and this nagging soon made inroads on Senna's peace of mind, and per-

The Car

As regards the championship events in general, and each individual race in particular, McLaren has always made it a policy to apply simple, single changes and to concentrate on maximizing the easy-to-drive function of its cars. The 1989 version of the MP 4/5 was also based on this policy, although the MP 4/4 - that dominated the 1988 season - outperformed the MP 4/5. As was traditional, the new car took a few turns on the Imola track before it was shipped to Rio for its debut. However, not everything went as smoothly as it had in the past. The car still looked youthful, but it

actually underwent some evolution during the year. Even those supposedly in the know couldn't make out whether this evolution was part of the program or was designed to provide a small effective margin of advantage over the others. This was supposed to be a completely new version, but it actually had last year's suspension system and transmission. After it had received a new front suspension, it got a new rear suspension, and finally - at Silverstone - the car got its definitive transmission. This continual evolution did not come free of charge because McLaren had to be content with the car not always being in tip-top shape. Fortunately, the Honda engine with its

high maximum horsepower and acceleration frequently came to the rescue in tight spots when McLaren's adversaries were snapping at its heels. The MP 4/5 is one of the few F1 cars today that make full use of the suspension travel, whereas all the other cars seem to have suspensions made of blocks of concrete. The McLaren sits rather high off the road. The movement is quite visible to the spectator, and the car's aerodynamic characteristics are consistent with its particular type of chassis. Apart from being beaten a few times by Ferrari and Co., the results have been very good. However, the MP 4/5 is still one notch better.

Tyrrell

The stability of this well-disciplined team - which is used to doing things systematically and in complete compliance with racing-management procedures - has established Tyrrell's image in the F1 world, an image that has remained unchanged through thick and thin, regardless of the particular drivers or sponsors. The '89 season saw the weakening of some of Tyrrell's institutional elements. In fact, the way Michele Alboreto was managed when Camel came into the picture as Tyrrell's sponsor left something to be desired.

Apart from contracts, legal actions and sponsor interests, a team's prime activity is supposed to be racing and the driver's only real passion to be driving, and this also means coping with the amount of personal risk involved. Tyrrell conducted itself with outstanding sportsmanship in the championship events and took admirable advantage of every available opportunity. This is one of this team's strong points, and its reliability permits it to reap benefits whenever a Grand Prix event starts weeding out its adversaries.

Tyrrell was also fortunate to run into Jean Alesi, that promising French driver. He wasn't supposed to race in F1 events this year but Alboreto's fall-out with Tyrrell opened that spot for him and he was in there racing even though his F1 debut came when the season

in a season where all the attention was being focused on the big name drivers who were battling it out for the title.

Tyrrell went into the season on a reduced budget - no sponsor but Ken Tyrrell had a new technical crew (all ex-Ferrari people). This made the crew a bit top heavy, but it also gave Tyrrell a big boost quality-wise and permitted a quick comeback to put the team back into the competition for the No.1 spot among those with cars not sporting "official" engines.

Then came the sponsors who were more-or-less post-Alboreto sponsors. It wasn't a big flashy season for Tyrrell - not like it was when Jackie Stewart was on the scene - but the development of new engines and the performance of the Pirelli tires (Pirelli's team package is being introduced to others with Tyrrell's experience) gives ample proof that '89 was a positive transition year.

The Drivers

One of the F1 rules is that only one change of drivers is permitted per team per year, except in very exceptional cases. Tyrrell, as well as certain other teams, have not stuck very closely to this rule. There were four drivers involved with car No.4. The first was Alboreto. The second was Alesi, but he wanted to win the

the old version. Then, using Michele's 018 in the race, he finished 5th the only decent "score" made all year long. At Monte Carlo, Michele and Ken Tyrrell had a heated discussion and the following Saturday, Michele also got his 018. He then debuted and came in 5th. He later placed 3rd at Mexico City, after which he began having problems with the crew.

On the other hand Jean Alesi proved that sometimes an unexpected break can produce a new champion. He debuted in France (his home territory) in Michele's place and right off the bat wins a 4th place. Other spectacular races follow, confirming his outstanding talent as a racing driver. Never getting riled or losing his cool, Jean gets along very well with everyone. You can easily see he's of Italian extraction, but his career (and passport) are decidedly French. Rather than having discovered this future champion, Ken Tyrrell just happened to run into him. However, Alesi may soon find that the present Tyrrell team fits him a little too tightly as far as his career plans are concerned.

was already under way. It was something right out of the blue for Jean because Michele Alboreto's position was actually untouchable. In fact, while still at the start of 1989, Michele's 5th place at Imola and outstanding 3rd at Mexico City proved how well he was able to hone his driving expertise in a Tyrrell car.

So, Ken Tyrrell snatched up this young talented driver, put him in Michele's prestigious vacancy and nailed him down with a 3-year contract. Jean was the only young driver of the season who disappointed no one as far as filling promises was concerned. And this was

Formula 3000 championship and vacated the spot which was then filled by Johnny Herbert, who had received his walking papers from Benetton. Fortunately, car No.3 remained faithful to Jonathan Palmer, who had just one moment of glory and then faded into the background for the rest of the season. The San Marino Grand Prix: the debut of the new Tyrrell 018. The 018 seemed like it had been specially conjured up for Alboreto; a unique car, a new version, out on the track factory-fresh.

Alboreto failed to qualify but Palmer did with

The Car

Having left the Ferrari behind them, Harvey Postlethwaite and Jean Miceot have worked hard to get the new Tyrrell 018 ready for the Grand Prix at Rio.

They didn't make it, but managed to get one ready in time for the Imola event, and another one for Monte Carlo.

The 018 design was quite obviously influenced by what Postlethwaite had been studying and realizing at Maranello before Barnard showed up and, as a matter of fact, before the former McLaren engineer had completely taken over the management of the engineering and sports activity at Ferrari.

This already advanced design was definitively realized at Tyrrell and, from its very debut, showed that it had several particularly effective features.

It's an essentially simple design with traditional nose streamlining and evolved rear-end streamlining, and a new overturned transmission which permits efficient weight distribution and is expecially advantageous on fast and medium-fast tracks.

When they first starting testing, they had a little difficulty getting the general tuning-up just right. When the car was delivered at Imola it still had assembly work to be done on it, and the mechanics still had to keep working right through official tests, and there were no funds available for any private tests.

These being the conditions, the potential shown by the 018 from the very outset continued almost unchanged all through the season. It's a very dependable car, and after the first few Grand Prix events the transmission had completely been debugged and they had no further difficulty with it.

With that car and that team, they were in a good position to win points, and they did every time they could.

What that car needs now is something better than its "private" engine.

WILLIAMS

This team was almost the favorite over Ferrari to give the powerful McLaren-Honda team a run for its money. Many expectations - especially those regarding the team's evolution throughout the year and the effort made by Renault with its re-entry onto the Formula 1 scene - actually had to be re-tuned because Williams adapted the 1988 chassis (already from the time of the Portugal Grand Prix) to mount the French manufacturer's 10-cylinder engine.

At the beginning, when all the other teams were breaking in their newly-announced weapons, the Williams team seemed to be a real threat. In fact, Boutsen and Patrese - with their double-header in the Canadian Grand Prix - made things look very promising indeed. The results were certainly good but not as good as those of the McLaren and Ferrari who put them in 3rd position at the line-up. The new FW 13 was way late in coming and the drivers complained that they were not competitive enough and lacked new aerodynamics that all the other teams already had out on the track. This postponed presentation of the new FW 13, Grand Prix after Grand Prix, was very hard on their nerves.

Renault probably figured it had lost a lot of time and had already missed out on the opportunity. Patrick Head, the team's chief designer and track manager, offered no particular explanation. The Williams-Renault

Patrese was going to be replaced by Prost. Everybody waited patiently for official confirmation that never came, and this made the team uneasy and lose some of its coordination. When Ferrari snatched up Prost, the situation calmed down and Riccado Patrese regained his usual easy-going manner.

With 15 world championship seasons behind them but with only three driver world championship titles to their credit (one would think they would have won more such titles), it seems evident that something's wrong with how these touchy top race car drivers are being managed. Are they being too straighforward and not using enough politics? This would be laudable on their part, but in the Formula 1 game this could be a handicap!

In the '88 season - with Mansell and Patrese (normally aspirated "private" engines) against the Honda turbos - any achieved positive result or world point was considered a gift.

The return to an official engine of the likes of the Renault had filled everyone with high hopes but at the end everyone was disappointed. Will the 1990 team obtain the desired results? That's what a lot of people are asking themselves. And this is what the Williams people are hoping with all their hearts.

The Drivers

Maybe the reason these two drivers work so well together is because there so dissimilar.

ticipation that would be hard for anyone to beat. He's always been a very determined driver and is still waiting patiently for that perfect season. Of course, besides being a very expert test driver and adoring racing, he also likes to experiment and is always at the team's disposal.

These are attributes that are even difficult to find in young unsuccessful drivers. The only thing that really annoys him is to fail to obtain what he figured he should have obtained from one of those advantageous situations that he's in the habit of creating for himself.

Although he's never lived in Italy Thierry Boutsen, a Belgian, acts and talks like a naturalized Italian. A nice chap, he's always ready and willing to cooperate in any way he can. Referring to his 1988 season with Benetton some say he's an opportunist. Opportunist or not, he's worked very hard this year and did well in several races, but perhaps Patrese got slightly better overall results. Canada was Thierry's best day. That sweet victory was an extra special present for him, as Riccardo knows so well.

team, therefore, decided to face up to reality and take '89 for what it was: a bridge to cross with things to learn along the way. In an atmosphere of expectation of a new car for next season, they buckled down to the job of learning. All the effort was applied in terms of the forthcoming year with the assurance of a Renault exclusive: two expert, very competitive drivers whose fervent desire is was to show what they could really do and get the track results they had long awaited.

At one point in the season it looked like

As far as team mentality and strategy are considered, both of them are first rate.

Riccardo Patrese and Thierry Boutsen may not be close friends but they've never had the kind of problems Senna and Prost (or Mansell and Berger) have had.

As a matter of fact, regardless of all the season's ups and downs, Patrese and Boutsen have always collaborated well together and obtained good results.

The 35-year-old Riccardo Patrese - a real Grand Prix veteran has a record of race par-

The Car

We should really talk about the highly-anticipated FW 13 that debuted in the Grand Prix of Portugal. It was not only fast but very reliable, at least from the standpoint of the chassis and the aerodynamics. As usual, this car also tends to be traditional and simple, which are the basic characteristics underlying all of Patrick Head's designs.

The suspension system is designed to be active; that is automatically adjustable in relation to the type of road surface, loading, and overall weight. The final design is still being worked out which is why the FW 13 still

mounts traditional suspension and why the dimensions of the chassis and body are greater than they actually need to be.

The car doesn't seem to have adapted very well to the characteristics of the various tracks, and the engineers have had to perform more tuning operations than were anticipated.

In the Grand Prix of Spain Riccardo Patrese actually outclassed his teammate by getting back behind the wheel of an "old" FW 12C; that is the '88 car that evolved into the FW 13 with the fitting of the Renault V-10 engine.

Situations of this kind can make people nervous if you consider that English teams are used to putting a car out on the track and

having it be fast right off the bat.

Besides being Frank William's partner, Patrick Head has the last word as far as design is concerned but he still doesn't seem to have adapted to the idea of evolution and design de-personalization, which is typical of such adversaries as McLaren and Ferrari.

One thing that still needs to determined is if there can be any synergy between the engine and chassis people; i.e. between Renault and Williams. In 1988 McLaren was right on target with its new Honda engine and followed through satis-factorily all through '89. The Williams now has to do the same thing and concentrate on development work next year.

It was the year of the Brabham's big comeback, the start of a brilliant season with hopes riding high with a lot of hope being put on the Pirelli tires.

Then right when Stefano Modena had resolved the pre-qualification nightmare by stepping up onto the podium at Monte Carlo, the team started running into difficulty. Performance dropped and so did reliability. The main problem was the lack of proper internal management compounded by economic and financial problems regarding ownership, and this made the future outlook uncertain. In other words, the team ran into a sea of troubles before their big comeback season was even over.

Maybe the two drivers were still a bit too "green" to be able to settle and stay up there. Furthermore those "unofficial" Judd engines ("unofficial" as compared with those used by the top teams) did not live up to their expectations. But Brabham was not alone in this. Bernie Ecclestone and Gordon Murray's former team - which has four world titles to its credit - was expected to take the role of an outsider.

The whole operation seemed a little off-key.

Whichever way you look at it, Brabham's record this year was something less than positive.

Using Pirelli tires was indeed an innovation, but it was also a gamble. At first it was Brabham who had the spotlight as regards tire performance, but this later switched to Minardi, the Italian team, and lights on Brabham dimmed down a bit.

Bernie Ecclestone has always been very strong about team management in the F1 world. He'd like to weed out some of the second rate participants but he hasn't considered that the "weeding out" could compromise the future of his former team.

The Drivers

Stefano Modena and Martin Brundle are as different as black and white and their careers have been likewise.

Brundle's had a couple of tries in the F1 game and both times he's been pretty unlucky; he never seems to have had the right car at the right time. He was at Senna's level in F3 in 1983 and drove for Tyrrell in F1 up to 1986. He

with his car's potential, as well as with his teammate's performance. Since people were expecting an awful lot out of Modena, Brundle's results were consequently viewed in a more positive light than would otherwise have been the case.

Stefano Modena and Senna both have the same amount of dedication to their cars and concentration behind the wheel. Like Senna, Modena really gets into the competitive mood before a race and in the pit he hardly notices what's going on around him. Sometimes doesn't even answer when someone says "Hi" to him.

There's, however, one small difference: Modena doesn't have a McLaren and this makes it difficult to really evaluate his real potential and just how much track expertise he's been able to acquire thus far. Both Modena and Brundle are confirmed as the drivers for 1990; that is, if the team is still around.

First there was Walter Brum, the Swiss; then Luthi, the wheeler-dealer financier; then the loss of the Alfa Romeo Pro-Car project; the non-definition of the 1991 Group C project; all followed by the defection of Teddy Meyer over the span of one Grand Prix.

When a team already has its hands full trying to cope with the championship and has to try to deal with "political" problems and figure out what to do next, it's really tough to conduct tests, race and promote stability.

then joined Zakspeed in 1987 and won the 1988 world driver championship for prototypes in a Jaguar. And now the 1989 F1 season doesn't seem to have given him much to look forward to.

He actually looked like he was going to be upstaged by Stefan Modena's performance. But Brundle was pretty good at not letting this happen.

He was fast in the test run and medium-fast in the races and his performance was consistent

The Car

This brand-new car, which has no connection to last season's car, isthe BT 58, in accordance with Brabham tradition, and made its first appearance in Brazil.

Its beautiful lines, simple appearance and flatfish aerodynamic configuration almost seemed to have incorporated a few of Gordon Murray's suggestions (before this engineer left Brabham after considerable thought to become McLaren's technical coordinator).

The Brabham had to go through the prequalifications. The cars didn't have a results record and therefore had to take one of the first four available spots in order to become one of the 30 cars participating in the Grand Prix.

No sweat. Both Modena and Brundle were very fast and hardly anybody could keep up with them. Pirelli was especially proud of their performance, because its professional reputation was banked on this comeback.

The BT 58, however, didn't evolve as it was expected to and pretty much maintained the same level of performance throughout the season.

The Argentinian engineer, Rinland, who was "captured" from the Italian team to manage the Brabham wasn't really able to do enough to help the situation.

Perhaps Rinland himself was penalized by the company's business management and couldn't concentrate and do his best work.

Quite a bit was done to improve the aerodynamic characteristics and the Judd engine was really up to snuff, but our impression was that Mr. Judd was not really dedicating himself 100% to the team, perhaps because he had too many irons in the fire or because he was thinking about what risks the future held for him.

This team started out with the kind of a budget only a top-class team would have. Their US sponsor - USF & G - invested quite a sum hoping to give the team a good boost, even though the cars used "unofficial" Ford-Cosworth engines. Of course, as far as engineering is concerned, this car can't match such super-engineered marvels as the Ferrari, McLaren and Williams but the hope was to sign a contract with a big company. The first objective was to get the "official" Ford engine which is Benetton's exclusive property, but this didn't materialize. But, all in all, the Arrows team didn't do badly. The impression we did get, however, was that the team wasn't really being managed with enough determination.

For example - and this seems quite strange - the new 1989 version of the A 11 was actually too small for one of Arrows' drivers: Eddie Cheever. And Arrows already had all the necessary data on Eddie regarding his body dimensions and weight before they started designing the car. By the way, Eddie is the only US-born driver competing in F1 events. And even now, with the championships over, certain races must be real torture for poor Eddie.

It's no fun when you have to use a lot of arm and leg muscles, braking, steering and shifting gears, and get a lot of calluses, sore spots, bumps and jolts. There's nothing that can beat a comfortable car that you don't have to fight every inch of the way. This has cost the team the loss of drivers and some of its better human resources. The team is therefore having to face a winter of reconstruction, of choosing the right drivers and furthermore is burdened with the unhappy situation of having to operate on a budget which is too low for getting the required results.

Arrows went through quite an exciting experience this year at Phoenix, with Eddie Cheever - a hometown boy - coming in 3rd to (frankly) surprise all of us.

This year's ups and downs prevented the team from really finding out if its problems were technical or organizational. They'll have a lot of work to do this winter.

The Drivers

Eddie Cheever had the satisfaction of getting up on the podium in Phoenix, his home town. The inspired winning of this 3rd place boosted his confidence but did not rub out the reality of a difficult year.

Eddie was fast and had plenty of guts, but he had such little freedom of movement inside the car that it rather cramped his style. His troubles began right at the outset. In fact, at Rio he had to drop out because of severe cramps in his legs, and from that time on he was never able to get the best performance possible out of the car.

Warwick, for his part, didn't do much better in his A 1l, but Eddie was left quite conditioned by this season, in which he had often had to fight to qualify and even didn't make it on a few occasions. So Eddie decided to get out of the Formula 1 and wait to get a better offer. Meanwhile, he's all set to race for Jaguar in the Group C world championships, and he may even get a couple of contracts to race in the Indianapolis events.

Derek Warwick, on the other hand, is sticking with the Formula 1, even though he too had a rather poor season, but didn't offer the excuse that the lack of driving comfort cramped his style.

Warick's been watching his years go by in the Formula 1 without being able to even prove to himself what he can actually do.

This '89 season with the A 11 did it. He's leaving Arrows to seek his fortune with another team.

It won't be a top team, but a Lotus type team that's looking for results that will boost its rating and would prefer an English driver.

The Car

In 1989 this English team and its American sponsor were supposed to become consolidated. Positioned part way between the A and B series, Arrows was figuring this year on presenting its A 11, a new vehicle conforming to the new regulations and aerodynamics. The A 11 was scheduled to make its debut appearance at the Brazilian Grand Prix. When Arrows designed the car, Eddie Cheevers was not being considered for '89, and it was only at the last minute - when it was too late - that they found out Eddie was too big for the car. It's hard to imagine, in this day and age, how such a design oversight could have happened.

So Eddie had to try to fit into a "cockpit" that was actually designed to take a man of Derek Warwick's size. This new car, however, did permit Arrows to maintain the position it had acquired the previous year; that is, right behind the various Ferraris, the McLaren-Honda, the Williams-Renault and the Benetton. These are the official cars, and Arrows showed that when you have a good frame and body design, even without the right engine, you can do some fairly good things but you can't be the protagonist all the time. Arrow's performance disappointed the sponsor who was expecting an improvement in quality.

No one will contest the fact this "English Ferrari Team," as it is sometimes called, is quite remarkable. The list of its numerous World Championship and Grand Prix victories is truly astonishing.

In the recent past, Senna has brought unusual honor to this team, especially as regards his performance with the car using the Renault engine.

This car was the protagonist of a team that seemed to have finally discovered its true personality.

Then in 1988, Nelson Piquet joined the team, and with him came the Honda engines, for which Lotus and McLaren had exclusives. Theoretically, McLaren and Lotus got the same engines, one for each of the Brazilian drivers on the two teams. The results of the '88 season were loud and clear, but those of the '89 season turned out to be even more so. The Judd engine proved mediocre, as did Nelson Piquet's performance, who was often even passed in test runs by his Japanese teammate, Nakajima. And even when he was ahead of Nakajima, it was only by a few 10ths of a second.

Everybody at Lotus were affected by this situation.

because of its poor performance record, and can't improve its performance record without the powerful, big-name engine.

Lotus was lucky enough to snag a sponsor that invested in Lotus and Nelson Piquet. Although Piquet has now left Lotus for Benetton (undoubtedly a step up for Nelson) Lotus doesn't seem to have any particular regrets. The team will use the '89 season for deciding how to best reorganize for the future, even as regards ownership. But it will bear in mind that drivers and engineers who are out to win races and make money can't be bothered with Formula 1 myth and tradition.

The Drivers

Satoru Nakajima has always been considered a good all-around deal, both as a driver and from the financial point of view, because he's quite popular in Japan and having him on the team automatically solves any sponsorship problems.

When Honda left Lotus at the end of '88, it helped relocate Nakajima.

Satoru Nakajima performed better in the tests this year than he did in the races. In fact, his

Doucarouge the engineer left, as well as Peter Warr the general manager, and Lotus spent the season getting set for the next one.

It just earned an odd point here and there, while Piquet seemed to be the only driver that could make it to the end of a race.

This is what always happens when a team doesn't have an "official" engine; that is, one made by a big-name automotive manufacturer. And, unfortunately, the strange situation is then created where a team can't attract the interest of a big-name engine manufacturer

test performances were the best they've ever been.

This Japanese driver is pretty fast and sometimes even faster than Nelson Piquet. He's built a good reputation for himself and the potential demand for him takes his excellent qualifications into due consideration.

He's greatly admired in Japan and actually a star there. The Japanese fans go wild about him. Although he's really refined his driving expertise quite a bit, he still hasn't been able to completely dominate his emotions during

the critical moments of a Grand Prix event; he still gets a little overexcited.

Nelson Piquet, on the other hand, has always been pretty cool and collected.

This year, Nelson gave the impression of just going through the motions, just to meet his contractual obligations. He wants a fresh start with Benetton, and isn't at all sorry about leaving Lotus. And the feeling is mutual!

It's no use making any comments about Nelson's technical performance this season. The Brazilian just seemed to be sitting back and sweating out what had turned out to be a bore for him. No doubt he comes alive whenever he thinks of Benetton, Nannini, Ford and, above all, Barnard!

He's got a pretty affluent life-style, the kind that you'd expect from a top-class driver. It remains to be seen if this aspect could play an important role in his future as a "salvaged" driver.

The Car

It's funny how so few people noticed the new Lotus 101 when it rolled out onto the track. Could it have been because of its yellow Camel color, or was it because the Lotus crew didn't attract the interest it used to.

Those in the business, of course, did notice the new car, while most of the general public did not. The new car doesn't have any substantial modifications over the old car and its performance characteristics are practically the same - still linked to the track characteristics because of the car's inate factors rather than because of how it's set-up.

Whenever there isn't any performance improvement, it's hard to say who's to blame: the driver or the crew. The previous problem, from the technical standpoint, was the Judd engine. It wasn't powerful and dependable enough. When he was developing the engine, Judd probably made some wrong decisions, and that compromised its performance.

Not having run any tests throughout the year, and not having the services of experienced mechanical engineers, it's no wonder the 101's evolution was only minimal.

Furthermore, private tests can only be considered useful if the driver performs as though he were competing in an actual race. Nelson Piquet must have given up right away, and the whole organization was automatically affected.

It's necessary to remember that some teams consider the Formula 1 a business, and their accounts have to balance.

Therefore, if you want to make development changes, run tests, and follow an up-dating program, you either have to have sufficient available cash, or be willing to invest a certain amount of money to get some victories.

march

We can still well remember the Portugal Grand Prix when the two McLarens were up front battling it out for the world's title, and right behind them was Ivan Capelli in his March. This Italian driver with his non-turbocharged engine was actually in a position to attack the turbocharged McLaren, the dominating car of the season. What a sad affair this 1989 season was! After the new cars were presented at Monte Carlo, the lack of performance and reliability throughout the rest of the 1989 season make it a season better forgotten than remembered. There were all sorts of problems, including drop outs, but one of the most dramatic and spectacular of all the negative events (which had nothing to do with the car)) was Gugelmin's take-off in the French Grand Prix in his March. He immediately thereafter wound up on his back with his wheels pointing upward. There was no doubt the March had everything going for it and could have been a protagonist in this championship series, and the ban on turbocharged engines was one of the factors in its favor. The March had already been checked out completely, more or less like the Benetton, and was in perfect shape to go after some important points. Cesare Gariboldi's passing was very strongly felt by the March team. He was a very good man, easy to get along with and very competent. Besides being a born leader and manager, he had been a real inspiration for the team, and will hard to replace. Their many problems included overhauling and race-preparation difficulties. March cars have always been very sophisticated, with advanced aerodynamic characteristics, and a very high ground effect as regards the body design. The car's typically inconsistent performance has always been conditioned by the track characteristics. 1989 was one of its most mediocre years in this respect, and when performance is down, problems come up. The drivers are unhappy and demoralized, the mechanics haven't got their hearts in their work, and nobody's pushing for improvement. Furthermore, the team's now fully owned by Leyton House (the Japanese firm), and this has probably helped cool the original relations between March backer Robin Herd and the Formula 1 team. During the Ronnie Peterson years (1970s), March was a protagonist. After which it took a three-year break and came back in grand style. But since then it seems to have taken a backward step or two, probably because of a combination of its innate characteristics and the engines. So, the slate should be wiped clean as far as this season is concerned, although the lessons learned should certainly be useful for the future. March's financial backing is as solid as ever; the team's got the same set-up it had in 1988 and 1989; and Ivan Capelli has received ample assurance that he'll be able to recover lost ground, and has therefore reconfirmed his faith in the team.

The Drivers

Ivan Capelli is no doubt March's trump card, and Robin Herd (the former owner of the team and its present design engineer) has complete faith in this Italian driver. In fact, with Ivan driving, the March won the 1986 Formula 3000 European Championship; and when March decided to switch to the Formula 1, Robin insisted on having Capelli on the team. Although he's only 26, Ivan's serious demeanor makes him appear more mature. He acquired a considerable amount of experience and professional skill while he was still quite young, thanks to Robin Herd. The '89 season was a bad one for Ivan, and he was quite demoralized by it. The only sure antidote for this would be a good season next year. He was even thinking of making a team change - taking a step upward, of course - and put his name in when Ferrari was looking for a young Italian driver with talent. But with Prost and Patrese also among the candidates, Ivan was fighting a losing battle. So, it was back to March to stay, hoping to have done the right thing and also hoping to get the kind of car he really deserves. His teammate is Mauricio Gugelmin, who is one month younger than Ivan and Senna's former student. He and Ivan are fundamentally different types. Mauricio is working on his F1 career with determination, but he's been a bit overshadowed on this team by Ivan's superior performance. However, this hasn't bothered him. He hasn't been jealous or begrudged Ivan's successes, as has unfortunately been the case with other teams. Mauricio Gugelmin's performance has been inconsistent. He knows how to get the best out of his car when it's in perfect shape. The trouble is, when his car's not in perfect shape. he doesn't know quite how to handle it. As a matter of fact, he's never given the impression of being a top-flight test driver. It may be that this friendly atmosphere and lack of rivalry between these two drivers accounts for the new March vehicle's sluggish evolution. Polemics should never enter the picture, but a strong sense of competitiveness within a team can be a great help sometimes.

The Car

In 1988, March came out with it very advanced 881, and everybody admired its very aerodynamic streamlining and large ground effect, which is the venturi effect that causes a lower pressure to be developed underneath the car, thereby allowing the air pressure from above to press the car down firmly and thus improve its road-holding and traction characteristics. The car performed very well and handled easily. There were some problems with uneven surfaces which made the car bounce a bit, thus destroying the ground effect.

The 881 also inspired the '89 designs of other vehicles. The present version is the Leyton 891, which was presented at the Grand Prix of Monte Carlo. Its lines are carried to a greater extreme, but the driver's arm movement was somewhat restricted because of the tight quarters inside the "cockpit." Any remedial action regarding this situation was an expensive proposition due to the one-piece construction of the body and upper part of the cockpit. Any such modifications would have required expensive mold modifications. The one-piece body and upper part of the "cockpit" design made it very expensive to effect any modifications, due to the high mold costs.

The carbon-fiber body, which is made in an autoclave under high vacuum, doesn't permit the flexibility required to make changes on the track site.

Both Capelli and Gugelmin found the new interior too cramped; that is, it wasn't comfortable. There was also some problems with the leg room, all of which led some to wonder if this problem of space had had a negative effect on the drivers' "sensitivity."

Therefore, it's rather difficult to properly evaluate the March 891. In any case, it was not competitive, not even in the trial runs.

This very light, tapered car was also penalized by its 8-cylinder Judd engine. It always ran very hot with accompanying loss of performance, and there were quite a few breakdowns.

So, everyone's looking forward to the 1990 season.

The Osella team could be compared to the Minardi team, although the Osella team had more construction, prototype and minor Formula experience followed by the big jump into the Formula 1 ten years ago. It was able to manage the Alfa Romeo turbocharged engine after Alfa had decided to interrupt the project. Osella's Alfa engines sometimes performed better than the Alfa engines themselves.

Osella went through a year struggling with a budget problem, but in that difficult and competitive Formula 1 world, it never failed to manage its team carefully and professionally. There were two reasons why 1989 was a difficult year. One was because the prequalification runs kept the team under constant pressure to make the starting line-up. The other was because Enzo Osella had promised himself that his would be an all-Italian team, including the drivers.

Larini, the youngest of all the Italian drivers (only one day younger than Alex Caffi), made his debut with Osella in 1988, and his improvement this year was quite noticeable.

Osella is undoubtedly very proud of Nicola Larini. When Ferrari called on him to stand in for Gerhard Berger in Mexico city (Berger was still convalescing), it confirmed the fact that Larini had become interesting for several other

onto a private track which is 1.7 km long. This track is too short for testing performance and aerodynamics. After having replaced a number of parts and completely reassembled the car, this track is just right for making functional checks.

Osella is one of the teams that Pirelli chose this year for using its tires, but Osella didn't always take advantage of the full capabilities of these tires. Things improved toward the end of the season, and the results matched those obtained by the other teams using Pirelli tires. There are some plans being made for the 1990 season. To a certain degree, the economic relationship between a team and a sponsor is not always a function of the number of times the team sees the checkered flag. It is sometimes affected by the dedication, devotion and seriousness applied to the development of a project.

The Drivers

Nicola Larini and Piercarlo Ghinzani are very likeable. Nicola is from Tuscan and quite young, while Piercarlo is from Bergamo and somewhat older, thirty-seven.

Nicola Larini got some good results and proved his worth on several occasions this season. The rumor was that he would be repla-

added tensions during the prequalification trials, Larini began showing some of the strain. But when Prost loomed on the Ferrari horizon, everything was put into perspective, and Larini could get a fresh hold of himself and do some serious driving. The improvement was quite evident. Whatever the future holds, Larini will be worth watching.

With Ghinzani, on the other hand, the whole picture was quite different. Though a fine driver, he sometimes just couldn't stand up under that prequalification pressure. It finally got to him, and he said that was it. When the season was over he was going to "hang up his goggles." Maybe if he got a good offer from some team that was more competitive, he'd stay with it. It's really hard to believe he'd quit cold like that, after being so dedicated to Formula 1 for such a long time. Of course, it's true he sometimes gave a little less than his best, 100 percent professional dedication, but, then, the Formula 1 game wasn't always all that generous to him either.

teams. On the other hand, the 37-year-old Ghinzani had nothing to show, and his season turned out to be only so-so. The qualification tires sometimes gave him some difficulty on the very fast test runs. Actually, as a company, Osella was a lot better organized than a lot of English teams. The shops at Brandizzo (near Turin) are laid out with a special department for each specific Formula 1 sector: chassis, engine, transmission, electrical system, body. The Osella chassis are custombuilt to Osella specifications by outside firms. The big door on the shop building opens out

cing Ferrari's ailing Berger, and Ferrari actually made it known that Berger's replacement would be its 1990 second driver. This, plus the fact that Ferrari announced it was only interested in a young Italian driver who showed some promise, cinched it; everybody was practically certain that Larini was in.

With all these exhilarating prospects, together with the thought that he was almost certain to be on the Ferrari team the following year (at the age of twenty-five!), it was no wonder Nicola began feeling a little cramped in his Osella. What with this excitement and the

The Car

This year's Osella car was called the "Fa 1/ M89," which we'll call "M89" for short. The chassis, which was designed by the Osella engineers, was built to order by an outside firm specializing in composite materials.

It's a well-thought-out design, which often results in similar cases where the necessary maintenance and overhauling after each Grand Prix event are taken into due consideration.

The M89 turned out to be more advanced than the previous model. Moreover, this time Osella made certain not to exceed certain limits as far as the aerodynamics were concerned, and made sure the drivers were going to feel comfortable behind the wheel.

Larini fit very comfortably behind the wheel, but Ghinzani was a little too husky to enjoy equal comfort.

There were some reliability problems with the car during this last year. They weren't structural problems, just little bugs that have the habit of eventually putting an F.1 car out of the race.

The best engine performance was obtained by Larini in the prequalification trials.

What really kept Osella down, however, was having to compete with cars like the Lola-Larousse (with its 12-cylinder Lamborghini engine), the Onyx (which is reputed to have a winning-team's type of budget), and the Ligier (which also has a great traditional type of budget).

All of Osella's design and evolution work was later tested on the track, but under the pressure conditions of the time and qualification trials.

BENETTON

Benetton's success in really being able to make a name for itself in the F1 world in just a few years is quite an accomplishment.

Benetton had a pretty tough year this year. It had placed all its hopes on Nannini, but he just didn't seem to be able to fulfill them as expected.

At the start of the season, there were objections on all sides as regarded Johnny Herbert, who wasn't completely over the injuries he had received in an accident. In fact, it was painful watching him get in and out of the car. During the early races even Nannini didn't seem to have complete faith in his team. There was a strange atmosphere there that seemed to persist even after he took the podium at Imola.

The fact of the matter is that there was some misunderstanding about what the deal was with Ford. Ford was the exclusive supplier of the 8 cylinder engine which was standing in for the multisubdivided 12-cylinder engine that Benetton was expecting to have in the near future.

The 8-cylinder engine arrived late, which set back the development and presentation of the new 189. Because of reliability problems Benetton had to make do with the old, bulky

materials. Then the hiring of Barnard was matched by the hiring of Nelson Piquet. Nelson may not be the youngest of the former champions, but he can certainly provide new motivations.

The hiring of Barnard, even part-time or even after Ferrari working hours, produced an immediate effect.

The Benetton reaped a fantastic victory in the Japanese Grand Prix. Admittedly, this may not have been a first-rate victory from the point of view of sportsmanship, but all through this race Nannini stayed in there with the best of them and even kept a close eye on Mansell. This would seem to mean that Barnard is already giving out intructions, even before starting on the overall reconstruction work.

The Benetton was out to win, and it finally did at the end of the '89 season, and wound up the No.4 team of the season. It has some pretty exciting ambitions for the near future.

The Drivers

Alessandro Nannini, class of '59, his first real driving job. Herbert was with him first, then came Pirro and then Benetton acquired an authentic Made-in-Italy atmosphere.

Japanese Grand Prix provided him with a big opportunity; and at the end of the season, Barnard provided him with that engineering reliability that he didn't have during the season. The right car at the right moment will produce the best moment in a driver's career. Nannini was taking the risk of missing that magic moment and not being able to capitalize on it. And since morale plays a big role in a sport such as auto racing, this '89 finale can turn out to be pretty important. Then we have Emanuele Pirro, who is Honda's test driver in Suzuka, who also likes to remember his F 3000 championship races in Japan.

Pirro had the opportunity to drive an apparently competitive car; and if Nannini was able to reap some glory, Pirro couldn't have been expected to do any better.

Pirro's experience will make it that much more interesting for him next year behind the wheel of another F1.

188, which also mounted the old 1988 engine. Benetton therefore not only had to battle it out on the track but also in the wings, working on agreements and programing.

However, all the desk work produced good results, and the hiring of John Barnard was the keystone of the future Benetton-Ford collaboration strategy.

This collaboration meant high-level Formula 1 industrialization, new shop and engineering facilities, new R&D facilities for developing new methods and sophisticated composite

Nannini came up from a season that was expanding and, in 1989, he was looking for his definitive consecration as a winner.

And he must have given it a lot of thought, especially as regards the new rules that privileged the non-supercharged engines: the "old-fashioned," time-tested engines that had the advantages on certain tracks provided by the limited fuel consumption of the 8-cylinder engines.

Alessandro Nannini obtained some fine moments, such as at Imola and England. The

The Car

Last year's car, the 188, kept the team going all through the first part of this season. There was a lot of talk about the new 189 car and the very powerful engine, despite its having onlyeight cylinders, but it was being held up because reliability problems were slowing down the test program. Then when the 189 finally arrived, its performance still left quite a bit to be desired, even though the improvement was considerable. The fact still remai-

ned that, under normal conditions, the McLaren, Ferrari and Williams were just too fast for it. Nannini had difficulty lending a hand in the evolutionary process because his teammate was not up to the situation. It was only after Pirro showed up that things got a little better. The car looks a bit "fat" compared to the thinner, more streamlined appearance that characterized all the other 1989 cars. The Benetton 189 also frequently had tire problems, which oftem forced Nannini to be the first of the top teams to make a pit stop for a tire

change. This car requires more evolution. It has less harmonious lines than do the Ferrari and the McLaren, and its supposedly simple 8-cylinder engine is complicated - both cosmetically and how it is mounted. It will undoubtedly evolve when Barnard gets there, but a completely new car will be a long wait. We've already seen how he's used to working. At Ferrari, his time schedules were certainly not cramped. So we shouldn't expect to see a 190 next year, but rather a 191 the following year.

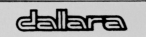

Scuderia Italia just wound up its second season. It's incredible. This club seems to have always been around, like the others who have contributed to Formula 1 history. And to think that only the year before, there was only one Dallara on the track, with Alex Caffi at the wheel, trying very hard to qualify, trying to get experience, and trying to have the team get some too. Available funding, the will to make it, seriousness in setting up the project, the immediate establishment of a racing image at a par with the best teams, are the things that permitted this team to break into the difficult and exclusive inner circle of the teams that really count.

The team approached the 1989 season determine to not let any opportunities slip through its fingers, because opportunities in the Formula 1 game rarely ever knock but once.

Andrea De Cesaris was hired as Caffi's mate, but there were a few things that had to be straightened out. Andrea, being a Formula 1 veteran, figured he should have the qualified car by contract to use in the official time trials, and that Caffi should have the second car (which needed to undergo the pre-qualification runs).

These problems were more a question of

such as when Andrea De Cesari came in third in Canada and his beaming expression on the podium was seen by millions around the world. Scuderia Italia was also giving the Pirelli tires a try to see if they were a valid alternative to the traditional tires used by the great teams. Even with the same kind of tire performance, how can one expect to compete with a McLaren-Honda or a Ferrari? Competitive tires can sometimes compensate for lower horsepower and the continual pretesting that the big teams do on all the championship tracks.

Scuderia Italia also had the Cosworth DFR 8-cylinder engine.

This year it looked as though Renault's interest in this team had been stimulated. There was the possibility that, besides the Williams, Renault was also looking for another team; but later on, it was clear that Renault had changed its mind.

So, Scuderia Italia - like all ambitious teams - is on the look-out for a larger, more powerful engine that will be more competitive than the traditional Cosworth. Meanwhile, Mr. Dallara will be going ahead this winter to plan the club's forthcoming third Formula 1 season along the guidelines of their development thus far.

ched the '89 season dead set on proving to everybody that those spurts of great performance he had in '88 were sure signs of the more mature Formula 1 performance they were going to see from him in '89.

Alex is a hometown, 25-year-old Brescia boy, and also a bit shy. Andrea himself is only 30, but has had quite a lot of Formula 1 experience. He's raced in 125 Grand Prix events and been on several teams, such as Alfa Romeo, McLaren, Ligier, Minardi and Brabham.

He's always been very aggressive and a battler, but recently he's been a bit more cautious and more predictable. A fast, no-nonsense type of driver, you never see Caffi trying to put on a show. He was with Osella in 1987 and joined Scuderia Italia while it was still in its infancy. Being so young and having shown he's got talent, Alex Caffi may have a bright future ahead of him, especially if Scuderia Italia manages to up-grade its performance like it wants to do.

personal prestige, and by about mid-season both had acquired sufficient points. A few great opportunities were lost, primarily because the impetuousness that both of these drivers are sometimes guilty, especially De Cesaris. They even got into each other's way a couple of times, such as in Phoenix when De Cesaris was passing Caffi, which resulted in Caffi winding up against the wall and losing a good scoring position.

But there were also some very fine moments,

The Drivers

This team put in quite a lot of time and effort to get the best drivers possible. First of all, it wanted an "all-Italian" image. The choice boiled down to either taking a young newcomer or Andrea De Cesaris. They finally opted for De Cesaris. He and Alex Caffi are altogether different types. Andrea was happy to join a serious team that wasn't laced with politics, where the atmosphere was conducive to doing something really purposeful. Caffi approa-

The Car

The technical structure of this team from Brescia includes the collaboration of a fine engineer, Gianpaolo Dallara.

The team's car - the BMS Dallara 189 - has evolved on the basis of the team's experience gained in the Formula 1, which began just last year. The design is straightforward, very traditional and based on previous concrete obtained results.

Gianpaolo came into the picture during the second half of the season. If he didn't have so many irons in the fire, he could have dedicated more time to Scuderia Italia, and the team could have done a bit better.

In fact, while the other teams that had the Pirelli did quite well, the BMS 189 wasn't able to get the most out of these tires on certain tracks.

De Cesaris and Caffi carried over their good winter performance into the first part of this season and often did better than the other teams at their same all-around level. Then their overall performance dropped off for a while, right about when the tires had begun to perform better, only to pick up again later near the end of the season, all of which demonstrated that the vehicle's "technical personality" was still inconsistent, and the team was still having to deal with some growing pains.

A lot of competition and effort is being applied by those not at the top of the list to develop cars that are fast, realiable and powerful enough to give the big boys something to really worry about. In this regard, Scuderia Italia can certainly take its place beside the likes of Tyrrell, Arrows and Lotus.

This a real "home-grown" Italian team, and everybody on it - the engineers, mechanics, etc. - put their hearts into their work.

This kind of sentiment in a racing team is somewhat of a rarity; and in this team's case, this behind-the-scenes sentiment really shows through. However, being something that is not forced or put on, but comes from the heart, it can only produce a positive effect on the team's professional results.

Minardi's been "in the racing business" for five years. When it was just starting out, its "Motori Moderni" turbocharged engine was a bit troublesome.

The team finally came into its own with the 1989 season, and got the kind of results it had been working so hard to achieve.

Actually, the full potential of the cars that Minardi had had in the past had never really been exploited, because Minardi's limited budget always made it difficult to get the right drivers.

The fact was that the up-and-coming drivers - like Alessandro Nannini - were inevitably attracted to the more competitive teams, or else the main sponsors themselves would practically force their choices onto Minardi.

In Nannini's case, he was like the promising managerial type who soon found that his little job in a small town couldn't permit him to

nized technical set-up, the new '89 car immediately proved to be competitive and dependable. Minardi's technical improvement went hand in hand with that of the Pirelli tires, which were originally planned for use by Brabham before Minardi was selected to use them.

Martini did some sensational driving in Portugal and Spain, especially at Jerez. He was first in the time trials by a long shot, and there were some very thrilling moments as he directly battled it out with Senna, Prost and the Ferraris.

There was no show of jealousy on the part of anyone, which went to prove that Minardi had earned everyone's full respect.

The team was faced with the problem some of the other teams were facing: getting an "official" engine. Both Minardi and "Motori Moderni" are linked to the Subaru Company.

With the whole Minardi staff eager to be protagonists, and Carletti's sound engineering skill and management, this may be an important turning point for the team.

The Drivers

Minardi had a good solid team this year. Sala, however, had a bit of trouble getting used to the new M 189 and the Pirelli tires. This caused some flaring up of temperaments,

perform spectacularly, and achieved certain levels that were brand-new for Minardi.

Martini is 28 years old, has only been in the Formula 1 for a relatively short time. He therefore still needs more experience before he can bear up under all that pressure the top drivers are used to.

Actually, his modesty and the straightforward way in which he talks about such important events as fighting it out, neck to neck, with Senna, makes him seem the antithesis of the classic protagonist.

This doesn't mean, of course, that a driver has to be arrogant to be a great Formula 1 driver. It's just that sometimes being too nice and courteous can make you forget that you really have to get in there and fight if you want to score. Otherwise you'll get lost in the shuffle. Both Minardi and Martini made a big leap forward this year, and everybody will be watching both of them in 1990.

develop as he wanted, and so he went to work for a big company in the city. The choice of Sala and Campos in '88 was 100 percent Spanish.

Minardi had a turn for the better during the previous year at Detroit when Campos was replaced by Pierluigi Martini who promptly scored with a 6th place and earned himself a world point. After that, the team was restructured around Martini, who was both fast on the track and a good test driver. After the reorga-

which was heightened by the "hot" entourage of Spanish fans.

Sala looked as if he wasn't digesting Martini's improving performance; it made him look a little weak by comparison.

However, by the end of the season, Sala had made a strong comeback, and the team atmosphere was again what it was always characterized as being: calm, pleasant and untroubled.

The fact is, however, that Pierluigi Martini did

The Car

The Minardi M 189 fitted the classic, "private" Cosworth DFR 8-cylinder engine which was modified and prepared by Mader. This traditional car developed out of the experience (even the negative) obtained during the 1988 season. In 1989, work continued to improve the aerodynamic characteristics, and considerable improvement was obtained. The car's air penetration and aerodynamic loading were increased without excessively decreasing its straight-line speed. The car had a good, but not excessive, ground effect. The use of the Pirelli tires, furthermore, nullified all past experience and required a whole new approach to the suspension system. The '88 Minardi had a suspension system that was as solid as a rock, but this year they got busy and did something about it, juggling within those few millimeters that the Minardi, like certain other cars, can be allowed to move when out on the track. When a Formula 1 car - which weighs about 500 kg - is loaded with fuel (about 160 liters) and its driver, there are only just a few millimeters' clearance between the car and the road. That's why the suspension system has to be so stiff. The Minardi M 189 is a lot like the McLaren, whose philosophy is that the suspension system should be as flexible as possible. In fact, the McLaren suspension system is the least stiff of any of the other Formula 1 cars. Evidently, all the engineering studies during the design phase, plus the testing out on the track with Pierluigi Martini's expert handling, made it possible to get the best out of the car, including the engine and the tires. A racing car's competitiveness is never the result of just one thing, but is the combined result of several factors, including the expertise of the driver.

The '88 season was the worst this team had ever seen in all of its entire history.

However, the changes made in preparation for the '89 season didn't give the impression of a completely new rebirth. Guy Ligier, the team's owner and manager, was there on the track in person, next to the pit wall. He explained to everybody that the team was in good financial shape. In fact, by contract with its sponsor, the team has unlimited financial backing until 1992. "What we need to do," he explained, "is reorganize our human and technical resources."

Renè Arnoux was still with them, and he got a very promising new 30-year-old teammate by the name of Olivier Grouillard (also a Frenchman). Some of the dead wood had been culled out (those who weren't willing to give it body and soul), and the team was ready to go. Their results weren't particularly encouraging, but Grouillard had brought a breath of fresh air and performance had improved. Of course, it wasn't so difficult to beat the previous year's record: eight races not qualified for, one ninth place in one race, and a total of fifteen dropouts.

The team lacked reliability; they weren't consistent. They did O.K. when it came to quali-

The Cosworth DFR engine didn't live up to its expectations, and it was not as reliable as it should have been, which was probably due to its having been mounted on a Ligier chassis. The team was also going through a technical identity crisis. Instead of devoting the time and effort to reorganizing his team, Ligier probably wasted a lot of it dealing with the associated legal problems after he had gotten rid of Michel Tetu, his former engineer.

When you look at the Formula 1 pits, you notice that those of the more competitive teams have neater and the crews are better. Moreover, the faster cars are more beautiful, cleaner, and more perfect. The Ligier pit and the cars themselves give the impression that the team's headed for the kind of glory they had at the time of Pironi and Depailler - 1979 and 1980 - a decade ago. Having put the '89 season away, Ligier now had his thoughts on the near future, but he knows that without an "official" engine, he can't hope to obtain a first-row line-up position.

The Drivers

Instead of an '89 profile, a whole book could probably written on Renè Arnoux. When a

usual. After 151 Grand Prix events, seven victories, eighteen pole positions, 181 world points, Renault, Ferrari and now Ligier, that was to be expected. He realized, however, that he still liked racing. It was that stress and heartless competition that had lost its fascination for him So, after this so-so year, he began looking forward to a more interesting year behind the wheel of a Peugeot Group C, putting all of his vast Formula 1 experience to good use.

Olivier Grouillard had a good season and his results were better than expected. He was definitely more competitive than his older teammate. And by the way he handled himself in both the trials and the races, it was hard to believe he was just a debutant.

Obviously, the F.3000 had been good training for him, and his more mature years gave him better judgment, but what his first year with Ligier demonstrated best was that he can also be competitive in the Formula 1.

fying, but then they made mistakes during the race, probably because the whole team didn't have enough concentration and determination.

Yes, there was a definite improvement in the '89 season that could very well continue onward in 1990. Renè Arnoux will probably be leaving the Formula 1 for the world prototype championships with Peugeot. Ligier himself knows exactly what he wants to do and how to do it. The feasibility of his objectives will have to be verified.

man gets to be 41, he's a little too old to be driving Formula 1, and - in a certain sense this was true in Renè's case, at least as compared with his younger 30-year-old teammate Grouillard.

It was the tires in the qualifying run that took their toll on Arnoux; that all-out lap with the cold tires where it's "all or nothing," where you can't gradually test to find the limits, but have to trust to luck that you're at the right speed whenever you take a curve.

It was evident that Arnoux wasn't as eager as

The Car

Compared to the real "disaster" that was the previous year's car, the JS 33 was a definite improvement.

Michel Tetu's chassis was completely replaced, but the JS 33 was still not competitive at any time during the '89 season. Replacing the Judd engine with the Cosworth cost the car a few horsepower.

Ligier wanted reliability, but the JS 33's streamlining didn't seem to be very efficient, especially in the side-radiator areas and air-discharge ports. Moreover, high running temperatures gave problems on the track.

Actually, the car's evolution during the year was not sufficient enough to keep up with the direct competition; that is, both pre-qualification and actual qualification competition.

This car was not built from a complete set of engineering drawings, and just sort of grew, piece by piece. It's drag wasn't too high, but its aerodynamics were rather limited. Ligier ordered wings mounted front and back to get the aerodynamic loadings that the body and underside weren't providing. Therefore, the JS 33 was somewhat penalized as far as speed was concerned, without having actually obtained good road-holding characteristics on the curves.

Grouillard did a better job of interpreting the car than did Arnoux. Most people in the business got the impression that Grouillard had the grit of a debutant and the enthusiasm of a driver who had reached the top rung of the Formula 1.

The McLaren-Honda has indeed won, but the Ferrari is something else again. All it takes is a Ferrari victory or any incident that involves the Ferrari in some way and journalists immediately push aside whatever they're doing and compose long articles on it. Senna has an argument with Prost and fifty journalists immediately hash it over. Mansell has a quiet conversation with Barnard and there are 200! This year the Ferrari showed up with a whole lot of innovations, probably more than any of the other teams. There was John Barnard's new F1/89 car, of course, and then the electronically-controlled semi-automatic transmission with the shift lever on the steering wheel, a new team manager (Cesare Fiorio, Lancia many-times rally champion), and finally there was Berger's brand-new teammate, Nigel Mansell, who was expected to do great, historic things for Ferrari. Moreover, the Ferrari was the object of a lot of criticism, both good and bad, all arising from the heft of the Maranello team, and pressure that was on it. Such pressure had never been experienced by the Renault in France. Whenever Cesare Fiorio merely moved his finger he was filmed, photographed and criticized. Mansell ignored the black flag and all hell broke loose. Mansell was lucky and won at Rio, and his name was on everybody's lips. He won in Hungary, and that was the turning point of the world cham-

ghout the season. A lot of time was wasted on that semi-automatic transmission, which stole time from the much needed testing that this new sophisticated vehicle required.
It was becoming the main topic in the pits. But Bernard stuck to his guns, finally made his point and got their attention. They might have gotten a couple of extra points and fewer drop-outs if they'd had a standard transmission. But they would also not have had some spectacular victories. This year's experience and evolution will undoubtedly serve the team well in 1990. What bothers them a bit is wondering just how much of a further jump of quality will actually be required. The question is: will the financial and other resources be enough without John Barnard there to coordinate things? They've got plenty of willpower, determination and grit, and the team has enough myth and legend to continue to carry it upward, even though there may be some low spots here and there. Prost's arrival has brought a new breath of fresh air, and it's doubtlessly also being fondly hoped that the atmosphere, as far as Prost and Mansell are concerned, will also be nice and fresh.

The Drivers

Nigel Mansell's arrival on the Ferrari No.27 got everybody excited. But then his adventu-

and Mansell were being just a bit too polite to each other, and that Berger was making eyes at McLaren. There was no doubt about it; all the eyes at the McLaren camp were soft and glowing for Mansell. No words were needed. However both drivers were very fast. Berger was exceptionally fast in the time trials, but was plagued with bad luck in the races (they say he used too much muscle with the transmission). At the end of the season, Berger finally got lucky and won, but behind that his sweet victory was the bitterness of having been so god-awful unlucky during the early part of the season. Mansell's head must have swelled just a little bit after all, because he insisted on being "No.1," and no arguments. Berger, of course, didn't need that, so he did what he had been planning to do anyway; he left, especially since Prost was hired to be Mansell's teammate for 1990. Now that'll be interesting to watch. While Ferrari would undoubtedly be happy to supply the high pedestals for these two kingpins, who's going to keep them from knocking each other over?

pionship. It seemed that wherever Ferreri went there was sure to be a good story.
Fiorio is to be given credit for having effectively consolidated the team. Anything that tended to reduce motivation was eliminated, and the team got back its fighting spirit and will to win. After being tugged one way and the other, Berger finally opted for McLaren and Prost. Perhaps McLaren's only serious mistake was to let Barnard slip through their fingers five years ago and join up with their competition that really needed him and had big plans. In '89, the team was on-again, off-again throu-

rous victory at the Brazilian Grand Prix in Rio, with Prost settling for 2nd place, put him up on the team's highest pedestal. He was just the kind of a "giant-killer" the fans were looking for, and they pulled out all the stops to let him know it. Berger's accident at Imola had focused all the attention (and hopes!) on Mansell. And with Berger down for the count, the (fickle?) fans - sad but true - showered Mansell with their admiration. No one was really coming out and saying that all that adoration had gone to Mansell's head (and that Berger had gotten a bit bitter), but the fact remained that Berger

The Car

The presentation of John Barnard's baby - the new Ferrari F1/89 - got a lot of attention and interest. This beautiful, very finely-finished vehicle had a number of brand-new mechanical and aerodynamic features, the most important of which were the electronically-controlled, semi-automatic transmission and the controlling mechanism for this system which was located behind the steering wheel. With this system the driver did not need to take his right hand off the wheel to shift. All he needed to do was move his finger. Ferrari was banking on this car to dethrone the McLaren.

Well, a whole book could be written about this F1/89 Ferrari. All the polemics, the initial unreliability and the transmission always breaking down (which prevented in-depth testing) monopolized most of the first part of the season. The transmission was supposed to have been a godsend, but actually turned out to be a ball and chain. Then things suddenly took a turn for the better. The transmission quit acting up and became the advantage it was expected to be, which made the car competitive. Its evolution into the next one will take place naturally, even after Barnard's left Ferrari. We even heard that other teams were also contemplating the possibility of adopting this technology. The end of the season saw a flare-up of the same difficulty: transmission unreliability. However, the '89 Ferrari definitely evolved during this last season. Its chassis was better than that of the McLaren, at least according to what the drivers say. Had it had a few more horsepower, it would have gotten better results. The fans are hoping they'll find this extra horsepower during the winter months.

This team is going through an identity crisis. After having a lot of technical and management difficulties, the 1989 season permitted the team to get that overall experience that they weren't able to get in the previous years. The relationship with the Lamborghini gave the team a boost in quality, not in performance but in technological professionalism.

Mauro Forghieri, the engineer who designed the engine, had all the telemetering equipment taken down to the track to check the engine evolution tests, just like the top teams do. It may also have helped to have had the telemetering equipment for the chassis and the aerodynamics. But they'll have that eventually; it's only a question of time.

The sound of the Lamborghini 12-cylinder engine was much appreciated by both the people in the pits and in the stands. Even the Ferrari was not able to "imitate" this unique sound.

The engine proved quite competitive on certain tracks, but had some difficulty on others, although it was difficult to tell in most cases whether the variance in competitiveness was due to the engine, the car, or both.

Reliability was also a problem throughout most of the season. One never got the impression that each member of the team was working in synergy with the others. There were requests between the Larousse crew and those in charge of the engine and transmission, but there was never an actual coordinated program being followed, as is the case of the McLaren and Honda, or the Williams and Renault.

At the end of the season, Larousse found a Japanese backer, and the team can thus now concentrate on becoming one of the top teams, like the ones that have official engines. The Lamborghini, in fact, is an official engine, but continual track tests will be required to obtain its maximum potential.

The team started out almost completely French, except for the engine.

Alliot and Dalmas, the two drivers, had a little difficulty at the outset of the '89 season, and weren't able to score at all for the first eight races. This made things grim: they had to pass the pre-qualifications before they would be allowed to do the qualification trials.

Dalmas never did make it and was replaced by Michele Alboreto, but that didn't change the situation noticeably. In fact, it seemed the team could only adequately manage one car and had to sacrifice the other. Alliot had already been selected for the sacrifice.

When certain external problems reflect on the matters concerning an F1 team, it's difficult to find the connection. The suicide of Didier Calmels, the co-owner and financer of the team, which occurred during the '89 season, penalized all the programs that were set up, thus creating considerable management and planning difficulties.

Since the financing of a team is even more important than its time trials and racing results, Larousse didn't waste any time or effort in looking for a replacement for Didier, which was finally found in Japan.

The Drivers

Yannich Dalmas didn't make such a mark for himself on this team. He was Didier Calmels' personal friend. When Didier committed suicide, that meant Larousse had lost its partner and financer. Besides the deterioration of his performance as a result of Calmels' death, Dalmas no longer had his personal backing. A combination of these two factors resulted in the termination of Dalmas' tenure with Larousse.

The 35-year-old Philippe Alliot had six years of Formula 1 experience and had always been a fast driver, but without having won many world points. The '89 season was a bit of the same. He was often aggressive and a fighter when it came to qualifying; but then in the races, he always seemed to have numerous problems that forced him to drop out.

Although things picked up at the end of the season, it was quite clear that Alliot had been somewhat stressed by the difficult atmosphere that permeated the team.

After his trying time with Tyrrell, Michele Alboreto was disappointed not to have found that relaxed atmosphere he was hoping to find in the Larousse camp.

Moreover, finding himself having to collaborate once again with Mauro Forghieri - with whom he'd had a difficult time when they were both at Ferrari - must not have been a pleasant prospect, especially when having to get through the qualifications.

Although it was sometimes said that Alboreto had the better engine, Alliot had even got ahead of him by as much as 10 km. Sometimes Alboreto would dismally fail the pre-qualifications, while Alliot would pass them with flying colors. This was a season for Alboreto that was hard to judge. The best that could be said is that it was a transition, and that the following season he'll be more concentrated and consistent. During the '89 season, Alboreto may not have learned very much, technically, but he's sure to have discovered that the Ferrari camp isn't the only one with problems.

The Car

Theoretically, the Lola LO/89 was built around the Lamborghini V12 engine, but the full potential of the assembly has never really been determined. During the early part of the season, Forghieri was continually complying with Larousse requests regarding clearances, mechanisms, tubing and progressions. The same thing occurred with the transmission and differential assembly, which had always been manufactured by Lamborghini.

There were moments when Mauro Forghieri - who has always been quite influential at Ferrari, and is even more so today - got a little irritated with these requests, because he felt than many of them were not necessary.

Then with all the instrumentation available today giving readings on all the functional parameters, it isn't very easy to pull the wool over anybody's eyes anymore.

There were actually cases in the past when Lamborghini felt it should take the responsibility for certain malfunctions or performance deficiencies. But if today's instrumention had been available then, it would have been revealed that the problems were caused by driver error, improper tune-up, or imperfect adjustment.

The LO/89 was interpreted very well by Alliot, but poorly by Dalman. Michele Alboreto also interpreted the car poorly. He always found it difficult to drive, and never easy to tune.

The chassis takes up a lot of space, and so does the 12-cylinder engine. The car does not have nice streamlining as do the more competitive cars, and the drivers have always had to fuss quite a bit with the wings to get the right aerodynamic effect required for obtaining maximum track speed.

Although the Lamborghini engine puts out a considerable amount of horsepower, the Lola-Larousse has never been fast on the straightaway, principally because of its technical factors.

coloni

The 1989 Formula 1 World Championship season saw Coloni Racing still struggling through its tough apprenticeship. It could be said that Enzo Coloni is, potentially, a young Frank Williams; that is, he's a spunky team manager who's willing to go to any length to make it in the Formula 1 "circus."

He's having the same tough time Frank Williams did when he was just starting out. At the end of its second Formula 1 season, the team was unfortunately still quite a long way away from any possibility of scoring. This team from Umbria was certainly determined enough. Right from the start - and for two seasons - they'd been doggedly trying to pass the pre-qualification and qualification trials and just score. But for the most part they were just going on hopes, because they lacked sufficient financial backing, without which no technical excellence can be achieved.

They were already halfway throught the season (the Canadian Grand Prix in mid-June) before Enzo Coloni could come up with a new car. His first driver, Roberto Moreno, failed to qualify four times before finally making it. His teammate, Raphanel, only managed make it

who headed the team and who had been wooed away from AGS at the end of the 1988 season. This was almost a mortal blow for the team and very negatively affected the possibility of developing the team's new car: the C3.

Unfortunately, having gradually slipped further and further off its schedule, plus the fact that there was no appreciable improvement in track results, results, there was little hope that the team could properly reorganize in time for the 1990 season.

At any rate, if Coloni does go into the 1990 season, his apprenticeship will continue to be quite grim. The only really substantial equity that Enzo Coloni can count on at the moment is his and his staff's raw grit and love for the sport.

Unfortunately (once again!) this is hardly enough for planning a dignified Formula 1 future. However, it wouldn't be wise to underestimate Enzo Coloni, because, a couple of years ago, he already seemed to have realized that what he had to do was just keep his hand in and wait until Lady Luck decided to smile on him for a change.

partially achieved, as witnessed, for example, by the good line-up position Moreno was able to get in Portugal, where he was ahead of the Benetton, Lotus, Arrows and the March. Unfortunately, this was the only bright spot in the season, because he never scored. Pierre-Henri Raphanel (the French driver) had been hired because of his sponsor value and not because he was much of a driver. He turned out to be a complete failure, and didn't do anything of note all through the season. At the end he quit and went to Rial hoping (vainly) to do better. His '89 record was highlighted by just one qualification (at Monte Carlo) and two or three accidents too many. At the final part of the season he was replaced by Enrico Bertaggia (from the Veneto area) who - being just a rookie - even had a tough time driving properly in the pre-qualification runs.

for the prestigious Grand Prix of Monaco, where, to everyone's surprise, both he and Moreno made the starting line-up (in their old 1988 Coloni cars).

Unfortunately, Moreno had obtained such poor results up to mid-season that his Coloni became subject to pre-qualification, from which he had been exempt up until the British Grand Prix. The very low budget that the team had to contend with all through the season caused the engineering team to leave, together with the French engineer, Christian Vanderplene,

The Drivers

Not even the experienced Brazilian driver, Roberto Moreno, was enough to give the Coloni team a boost in quality. Moreno was the 1988 Formula 3000 champion, and before becoming a driver with Coloni, he had been with Ferrari as a test driver, and had given his all trying to develop the car that had been put at his disposal.

Through no fault of the crew or the driver himself, the objective with Coloni was only

The Car

Enzo Coloni came out with two cars during the '89 season. His financial situation delayed the presentation of his new C3 until mid-season. This car was only in the design phase at the beginning of the season.

So, Moreno and Raphanel had to made do with a modified version of the old FC 188 for the first part of the season. This was the car Gabriele Tarquini had used the previous year, and he always had a tough time even making

the starting line-up. So, actually there wasn't too much that could be expected out of the "modified" FC 188 used in the first half of the '89 season. Everybody was really flaggergasted when they saw both of these 188B's out there on the starting line-up at Monte Carlo. The new C3 made its debut in the Canadian Grand Prix, and Moreno had no great difficulty qualifying for it.

But that just turned out to be a short-lived success, because shortly thereafter the C3's French designer, Vanderpleyne, and Colini

parted ways, and that affected the further development of the car. It wasn't until the British Grand Prix that Raphanel was able to have the C3, but this former Formula 3000 driver soon left the driver's seat vacant for Bertaggia.

The C3 had a beautiful, streamlined body (the 188B looked like an armored car by comparison), and it was a pity Vanderpleyne couldn't have stayed on to develop it completely. However, the C3 provided a good base for future development.

It takes more than a Japanese engine to make a racing car great.

Eric Zakowski (a Polish refugee and Zakspeed's owner) found this out at the end of the '89 season - as also did his drivers, Bernd Schneider and Aguri Suzuki - because the German team's balance sheet was heavy on the negative side.

The two Zakspeeds hardly ever got past the pre-qualifications. In the two Grand Prix events that they were able to race in, Schneider had to drop out after only a few laps.

So not only was the competitiveness of the cars not put to a test, but it never found out just what the 8-cylinder Yamaha engine could really do. After watching one race after another go by, the Zakspeed-Yamaka combination appeared to be more of a badly mixed cocktail than a technological joint venture capable of keeping company with the Formula 1 greats.

Last year this little team from Niderzissen was actually in its fifth Formula 1 season, but it still didn't seem able to make the grade. Of course, it should also be noted that Hamamatsu's 8-cylinder engine has never really impressed anybody very much.

The Yamaha Co. is certainly not the Honda Co., but its engine designers - such as Yoshi Kawa - may still have some surprises that their typical Oriental humility has kept from being predictable.

The team and Yamaha are still both hoping to get some good results and have therefore decided to continue with their association. So, 1990 may very well be a decisive year for them.

Unfortunately, Zakspeed and its partners are going to be handicapped by having to undergo the prequalification tests, which were the main reasons for their having made so little progress during the '89 season.

At any rate, the credit for the seriousness and professionalism of the entire Zakspeed team all through the '89 season goes, without doubt, to Eric Zakowski. There was no merry-go-round of drivers on the Zakspeed team as there was on other teams that were desperately trying to score. Zakowsky was smart enough to think well ahead during the winter, thus assuring that he'd have an adequate budget.

If anything, his problem would concern having drivers that aren't quite up to the job. Bernd Schneider has the strong backing of the West Co, the team's main sponsor, and Yamaha has insisted on Aguri Suzuki as the second driver.

Moreover, Zakowski has guaranteed that the Japanese engine man will have a first-class engineering staff. One only need to remember that the ZK 189 that participated in the world championships was designed by such engineers as Gustav Brunner and Nino Frison, who were "stolen" from Rial's rivals during the winter.

The Drivers

The '89 season - for both of the Zakspeed drivers, Bernd Schneider and Guri Suzuki - should be rubbed off the slate. Bernd Schneider was only able to participate in two Grand Prix events: the one in Brazil and the one in Japan. Aguri Suzuki never even got past the prequalifications (and he's Yamaha's "fair-haired boy").

It was pretty obvious that neither of these two drivers were up to the job assigned to them. After all, both of them are still little more than rookies in the Formula 1 game, and they had far too little experience to have been able to properly tune an engine that had never previously been mounted on an Formual 1 car. So, Schneider's previous total of six race participations only be two more.

In Brazil, he went thirty-six laps, while in Japan - after having given the Yamaha people a thrill by qualifying right on their own home territory - his transmission went out after just one lap.

Suzuki did worse than that. After his positive debut in 1988 at Suzuka with the Lola, he figured he really didn't have to go to all that trouble, and just watched the Grand Prix race from the pits.

The Car

The ZK 189 was designed by Gustav Brunner and Nino Frison, two top automotive engineers. The car showed good promise for the '89 events, but turned out to be a disappointment. It only participated in two races. The strange part was that a great deal of care was put into the design of this car. The well-tested Yamaka engine had made its successful debut at Jerez in December of '88. After that, the Japanese-German team had put it through a series of severe tests on tracks all over Europe, from the Vallelunga to the Paul Ricard.

Perhaps the constant Grand Prix appointments and the burden of having to face the prequalifications was too much for Schneider and Suzuki, and they couldn't concentrate well on getting the best possible tune-up on the car, whose design was also probably a little too complicated for the capabilities of the team.

Brunner and Frison had kept the size of the car down to an absolute minimum. It was very narrow, and the 75[inclination of the Yamaka engine permitted a very sharp slant in the nose, which was thoroughly tested in a wind and rain tunnel. Unfortunately, the well thought-out design and subsequent winter tests were not adequately followed with development tests during the season, and this was reflected in the poor results that were obtained.

Mike Earle's Onyx team was the most ambitious of all the teams making their debut in the 1989 Formula 1 racing season. This is justifiable, considering Mike's outstanding staff and substantial financial backing. For a number of seasons, March had chosen Onyx as the official Formula 2 and Formula 3000 team, in which it logged such an impressive number of successes that it couldn't help but move up into the Formula 1 category sooner or later. When it was in Formula 2, the backer was Moneytron, the Belgian finance company owned by the eccentric billionaire Van Rossem, who personally promoted the promising young driver Bertrand Gachot.

With his ample budget, Mike Earle was able to affort such a man as Alan Jenkins, the outstanding design engineer who had made quite a reputation for himself, both in the Formula 1 and in connection with the Indy car CART Championships.

The pre-qualifications gave his drivers some difficulty, with Gachot taking seven trys to break the ice and debut, which was in France. The more seasoned Johansson (who made the podium in Portugal), had no particular problem and even continued to improve his

builders, Onyx won't have to worry about the 1990 prequalifications, and this is further proof of how extremely well this British team did. And its ambitions for 1990 season are no secret to everyone.

Since all the factors that made Onyx the "debutant of the year" were again confirmed, their future success is therefore assured.

Right after the last 1989 Grand Prix race in Australia, Earle and his crew were back in Sussex, laying out the program for the winter, in preparation for what is sure to be a decisive year in a adventure that very propitiously started off with the right foot.

The Drivers

Jurki Jarvi Lehto Stephan Johansson had just finished his disappointing seasons with the Ferrari and the McLaren, and his horrible season with Ligier! So he was the last one to suspect that he was going to have such a good season with the Onyx.

This blond Swede from Vaxjo successfully hurdled practically all of the prequalification runs.

with Onyx and didn't have much experience, which meant that Johansson had to do all the delicate development work on the car for that year.

Therefore, it was only natural that he should be allowed to reap the benefits of his work in 1990.

But despite his lack of experience, Bertrand Gachot put in a good season and proved he belonged in the Formula 1. Too bad his falling out with the team near the end of the year compromised his future.

His replacement was the Finn, Jyrki Lehto, who was also confirmed for the 1990 team.

track performance right through the season. In recent years, very few brand-new Formula 1 teams have obtained such good results, thanks to its good organization and high professional level.

Earle wanted this because he knew they could make a good impression their first year out. (One should remember that a few years ago, the team had already contemplated the move, but didn't.)

Having placed well in the world events for car

But Johansson's most rewarding day came in Portugal when he barreled in behind Gerhard Berger and Alain Prost to take third place.

Almost two years had gone by since he had last climbed up onto a podium (when he came in 3rd in his McLaren at the 1987 Japanese Grand Prix).

But even before this third place at Estoril, he had already been confirmed on the team for 1990.

His 1989 teammate was making his debut

The Car

In just nine months - from when Johansson flubbed twice on the Brazilian qualification runs (late March) to the day he won his 3rd place in Portugal - the Onyx Ore 1 had made a surprising amount of progress.

Equally sharing all the credit were Alen Jenkins, the design engineer; the drivers, who had put the car through it best paces both in the time trials and in the races themselves;

and, of course, the pit crew. As a matter of fact, the team's overall efficiency was so amazing that many people actually forgot to take a good look at the car's very interesting engineering features.

Jenkins was fortunate to have been amply funded, because this allowed him to work unimpeded and extend his design ideas beyond the limits of the ordinary, tried-and-true, conventional type of design that the other new teams preferred. For example, right

at the start of the season, he had a transverse transmission mounted on the car, just like the one on the McLaren.

Moreover, the car was esthetically outstanding in every detail, so much so that it was considered one of the most beautiful cars of the '89 season.

The track results proved how well the car was engineered and built. In fact, an evolution of the Onyx Ore 1 is slated for the first Grand Prix events of the 1990 season.

trials during the previous year was quite good. In an elimination race at Detroit, De Cesaris came in a prestigious fourth, the importance of which was better appreciated later on when it permitted the Rial team to be partially immune from '89 pre-qualifications. All of these wonderful results must have really gone to Guenther's head, because he decided to use two cars in '89 instead of one. In a decidedly all-German vein, he assigned Christian Danner (a nice honest driver, but nothing more) to one, and Volker Weidler to the other. Weidler was a young promising Formula 1 rookie, but had been disappointing in the F.3000, even though he had had the use of an official car). To further complete the picture, Gustav Brunner left the team. He was a former Ferrari engineer who had designed the car that De Cesaris drove in the '88 season. Considering all these facts, it's easy to understand how Rial was almost always at the tail end in the official trials. However, notwithstanding all of this, Guenther Schmidt's team seemed to have had Lady Luck on its side, considering the fact that Danner copped an incredible fourth place at Phoenix, thus saving the second car from having to submit to the pre-qualifications. America obviously brought the team good luck, what with Andrea De Cesaris also having (partially) removed the pre-qualifications specter twelve months earlier with his fourth at Detroit. So, the little team's good luck in Arizona sensationally saved an otherwise poor season, and also provided yet another example of how unequitable the system is for deciding who has to undergo pre-qualification and who does not.

The Drivers

In all, 5 drivers got behind the wheels of the two Rial cars during the '89 season (including Thomas Danielsson, the Swede who only did only one run in the Hockenshiem Goodyear tests). The most expert and loyal driver of this happy bunch was Christian Danner. He was the only one to qualify the Arc 02, and the only one who left a good impression before leaving the team (by getting a 4th place in the U.S.A.), which he did following the Grand Prix of Portugal.

The other German driver, Volker Weidler, was laid off unceremoniously after the Grand Prix of Hungary. He didn't even get a chance to debut. Raphanel, who had done a lot of hard swallowing with the Coloni team and was eager to see what he could really do, took over from Weidler. Then, in Spain, Foitek joined the team, but his accident during the official trials convinced him that was no place for him. Then we had Bertrand Gachot, who had left the Onyx team. How come all of this coming and going involving such an insignificant team? Simple. They were attracted by the mirage of becoming one of Guenther Schmidt's "chosen ones," so as to be able to avoid the prequalifications hatchet (although none of them ever even saw the starting line).

Every year, there's always one team in the Formula 1 World Championship Series that has to be content with trailing along way behind and "bringing up the rear."

In the '89 season, it was the Rial team's turn to play this ignominious role. This German team grew out of the ashes of the ATS team (which left the scene at the end of 1984) and is headed by ATS's former owner Guenther Schmidt. Schmidt is a high-powered German businessman who's got a penchant for the Formula 1, who's made quite a name for himself in the sport, mostly because of his tyrannical behavior and exaggerated ego. In 1988, after a three-year pause, Schmidt decided to get back into the Formula 1 game and, to be perfectly frank, his team looked quite promising, thanks to a spunky Roman driver named Andrea De Cesaris. Although the team had a reduced staff, its performance in the

The Car

Rial's failure in the '89 season was due to its unsound technical basis. Gustav Brunner had practically done miracles by designing a car that was not only reliable but even sometimes quite competitive, and all on little more than a shoe-string budget.

When the team lost Gustav they had to try to make do with the shy, retiring Stefan Faber as their chief engineer. There was nothing else he could do but try to rework the Arc 01, the '88 model.

The Arc 02 was the result, a very traditional car with very few new features (longer body, new suspensions and reworked transmission) and with very few development possibilities, as was demonstrated as the season progressed.

While other teams were improving, Rial seemed to be stuck right there at the same point it was at the start of the season. Christian Vanderpleyne - Coloni's former engineer - tried lending them a hand, but even that didn't seem to help. What really made development difficult was the continual change of drivers and their lack of experience.

The Arc 02 was consistently the slowest of the lot and, of course, very non-competitive. Near the end of the season, the car began to have some structural failure (probably due to metal fatigue). For example, Foitek lost a wing at Jerez and had an accident.

The '89 season turned out to be a series of ups and downs for this French team (from Gonfaron) managed by Henri Julien. Unfortunately the "downs" outnumbered the "ups." Bad luck hit them right off the bat during the free trials that preceded the first Grand Prix event, which was in Brazil.

It was the team's Parisian driver, Philippe Streiff, who had the tremendous bad luck when his car went off the track at very high speed and seriously injured his spine, so much so that he's still confined to a wheelchair. It seemed that the car's roll bar broke loose, which resulted in Streiff being injured so seriously.

The team took this loss very hard, and their morale plunged even further because they had to start off the season with the old '88 model and only one driver, Joachim Windkelhock, a rookie who was making his debut. Their moral got a lift when they were able to hire Gabriele Tarquini, who started with the Imola race and gave AGS its best of the season.

Tarquini was happy to get back into the Formula 1, after thinking for a while there that he was going to be left out. So, he enthusiastical-

ly went to work and made a good showing for himself at the Monte Carlo trials and in the Mexico City race.

These results, however, didn't relieve the team of having to go through the agonizing pre-qualifications. Performance began dropping off at about mid-season. Not even the new car (it was ready in August) nor the hiring of Yannick Dalmas to replace the inexperienced Winckelhock was enough to stem the tide. AGS probably lost its chance to make a real jump in quality when its No.1 driver,

Streiff, had that terrible accident. In fact, in that brief instant, on that March morning in Rio, all of AGS's strategic plans - which were hubbed on Streiff - had been wiped out in a cloud of dust.

After all, Streiff was AGS's standard bearer, and all the team's future hopes depended on him.

Unfortunately, the team's woes were further aggravated by rather serious technical problems. Having been a bit too pleased, perhaps, with the spring results obtained with their JH 23 (which mounted a Ford engine), they put off presenting their JH 24 (which, in any case, was not a car that represented a definite step forward), and this prevented Tarquini and Dalmas from being able to save the season for them.

The Drivers

The AGS team used a total of four drivers during the season. Streiff, the No.1 driver, had run all the winter tests. The team would have undoubtedly done better if it hadn't lost Streiff right at the start and had to make replace-

ments for him and for the rookie, Joachim Winckelhock.

The best results were obtained by Gabriele Tarquini. Just a few weeks before joining the team, he had no F1 engagement and was getting a little desperate. And he was very happy to get behind the wheel of a competitive F1, as was the AGS car at the beginning of the season.

His first race for AGS was at Imola where he came in eigth. If Williams and Dallara hadn't succeeded in removing Boutsen and Caffi's

disqualification, Tarquini would have placed sixth.

So, Tarquini won his first world point just two Grand Prix events following the one in Mexico City. His '89 record also includes a nice fifth place at the end of the first day of trials at Monte Carlo. After that he was overcome by the trials and tribulations that were afflicting the team.

Yannick Dalmas joined the AGS team in time for the British Grand Prix. He had been fired by Lola-Larousse and was eager to make up for this. But even with all this determination, he too was negatively affected by the team's problems and could do little to help. Winckelhock was never able to even prequalify, and he was replaced right after the French Grand Prix, so it would be difficult to say if he had any real driving talent.

The Car

During the '88 season, Philippe Streiff in his JH 23 (which mounted a Ford engine) performed quite well during the trials, but the car was exceptionally unrealiable in the races. This situation didn't improve much in '89, although the use of an evolved version of the old model to start off the season did give Tarquini a chance to get some preliminary results.

But, as often happens, there was no development work done, and this caused a bit of confusion among the technical staff of this French team.

The new JH 24 made its track appearance for the Goodyear tests at Silverstone, and was officially presented in the qualifications for the French Grand Prix.

However, the JH 24 never actually got a chance to make its racing debut, because neither Tarquini nor Dalmas (who only got the

car in Belgium at the end of August) were ever able to make the starting line-up. In fact, it only happened just once (and only with Tarquini) that the JH 24 was even able to get through the pre-qualifications. But, after all, what could one expect from the evolved version of an '88 model?

The JH 24 substantially had the JH 23's body (with roll-bar and side modifications), a new engine hood, revised rear-end aerodynamics, and a slightly longer wheelbase.

The results obtained by this team in 1989 were quite demoralizing. They didn't make it once in any of the starting line-ups. They got just a little encouragement in one instance when, in Brazil, Gregor Foitek got past the pre-qualifications in his ER 188 but didn't get into the line-up.

In the second half of the season, Oscar Larrauri for Zurich took over from Foitek, and even he wasn't able to make it. Although he had a new silver-colored car to drive, he never ever got past the Friday morning lottery.

This Swiss team, managed by Giampaolo Pavanello, just couldn't get competitive. Well, they hadn't done much during the winter. They only went out on the Monza track a few times, and they showed up in Brazil with a modified version of the previous season's car, the one with which Stefano Modena and Oscar Larrauri had had difficulty in keeping up with their nearest opponents.

When Gregor Foitek fell out with the team, he accused the car of being technically inadequate, but it was Foitek's technical inadequacy that prevented the engineering team (headed by George Ryton) from being able to properly tune the car to meet the require-

do one or two little things that were rather significant, the '89 season was made more complicated by the appearance of nine new teams, all of which were in better financial shape (such as the Onyx). This boom in the number of new teams signing up for the F.I world championships was very tough on Eurobrun, AGS, Osella and Zakspeed, because they weren't able to participate in any of the races held during the '89 season; a veritable record, in the negative sense. All the other so-called "teetering" teams were lucky enough to avoid this fate.

The new Eurobrun car unfortunately only became available late in the season (German Grand Prix), and Foitek and Larrauri had to put it through its paces in the Friday morning prequalifications, instead of being able to concentrate on the getting the right time performance for being able to participate in the official trials. In other words: a hopeless situation.

The Drivers

All Formula 1 drivers have to face an arduous

also a big disappointment (he had a terrible accident during the free Friday morning trials), which made him decide to give it all up, at least for 1989.

Aside from all the bad luck, it didn't appear that Foitek could actually be included in this decade's small group of champions.

Oscar Larrauri, a very nice Brazilian fellow and former Formula 3 champion (1982), made his return to the Grand Prix world almost without being noticed. This took place at Monza in September.

The previous year at Eurobrun he had greatly disappointed his teammate Stefano Modena. His decision to try to make it in the '89 season behind the wheel of the ER 189 was probably ill-advised, because out of five trys, he racked up five failures.

ments. The Eurobrun team seems to completely lack motivation and enthusiasm. Of course, having to try to obtain results when working on a very restricted budget is something that would even take the enthusiasm out of the most rabid Formula 1 buff.

As with all the other teams that had to undergo the prequalifications, the Eurobrun team was also denied the opportunity of obtaining valuable racing experience. Even though Eurobrun had managed by some miracle in 1988 to

task when making their debuts, but the 24-year-old Swiss driver, Gregor Foitek, found his first season in the F1 "circus" absolutely nerve-racking. This former F.3000 driver got only one chance to face the official trials in his Eurobrun. This was at the first Grand Prix date in Brazil.

In the ten dates that followed, Foitek had to give up after every one of the Friday morning prequalifications.

His shift over to the Rial team in Spain was

The Car

This Italian-Swiss team addressed the '89 season's early trials with a modified car from the previous year. This car was the one Stefano Modena and Oscar Larrauri had used, and the modifications included a new chassis and transmission, and all aerodynamics had been revamped. As the '89 season progressed, no development work whatsoever was done on the car, and unavailability of useful results caused the debut of the ER 189 to finally take place in Germany. The car was designed by the British engineer, George Ryton, who used to work with John Barnard at GTO. The main feature of the ER 189 (which was Ryton's first Grand Prix design) was the suspension system. Strangely enough, this system was very similar to the one on the '89 Ferrari, which caused no small amount of accusations and criticisms. But Ryton was not only inspired by the Ferrari suspension system, but also got some suggestions from the McLaren, especially as regards the shape of the engine hood. The rest of the car design was quite conventional and in keeping with the budget available for its construction. Unfortunately, not even having a new car to race with managed to change the situation. When the new car was finally available, late in the season, its performance was disappointing. In fact, it never did get past the pre-qualifications.

This is the so-called "pit walk" when the general public is allowed to visit the pits during the breaks between practice sessions. At any other time, the pits are off limits to any visitors except top brass and VIPs.

A look at the wheels, once gone off track.
(following page)

The Ferrari's semi-automatic transmission was supposed to be its secret weapon and did indeed prove to be an important technological innovation. However, the bottom line was that it proved to have more disadvantages than advantages.

(opposite)

These are Nigel Mansell's hands with which he so ably managed the Ferrari and its semi-automatic transmission. His hands are given the credit for his having won the race at Rio! They were later bleeding when he grabbed the winner's cup a bit too energetically and cut himself on a sharp corner.

At the Phoenix track, moments after take off.

Bertrand Gachot, this driver from Luxemburg who - of course - fondly believes in a united Europe, grew up in Belgium and perfected his racing in France. His career's shot upward like a rocket. After only two months with Formula 3, he "graduated" to Formula 1.

Gerhard Berger's gaze is intense as he completely concentrates, seconds before roaring off down the track to try to win that coveted pole position, no mean trick when you're battling against a fast, determined and intrepid driver like like Senna in his highly-competitive McLaren-Honda.
(opposite)

Dreams faded at dawn, a morning try out brought no reward.
(*preceding page*)

Drivers' lives are in the hands of these complicated wheel hubs and technologically-advanced brakes of the Formula 1 car.

Tire changing: one of the most exciting moments in a race, where the final outcome could actually be on the line.
The mechanics here are changing the tires on Mauricio Gugelmin's March.

"Lift by strap only", precise instructions for car lift-up.

This ballet would seem to halt the legend that Formula 1 is populated with beautiful girls. Up to about 10 years ago women were more in the forefront. Now the extreme professionalism of the environment has moved them to a non-protagonist role, although there are still a considerable number of them in the paddock.

Renè Arnoux at 41 is the oldest Formula 1 driver. He made his debut in the world championship series in 1978, and has driven for Martini, Renault and Ferrari. Now he's defending the Ligier colors.

The Phoenix airport is located inside; a city landing, a desert view.
(following page)

Nelson Piquet's Lotus seems to have risen out of the hot Phoenix asphalt. But this season that has just closed was not so hot for either our Brazilian driver or the prestigious British firm that - not too long ago - was being referred to as the "English Ferrari".

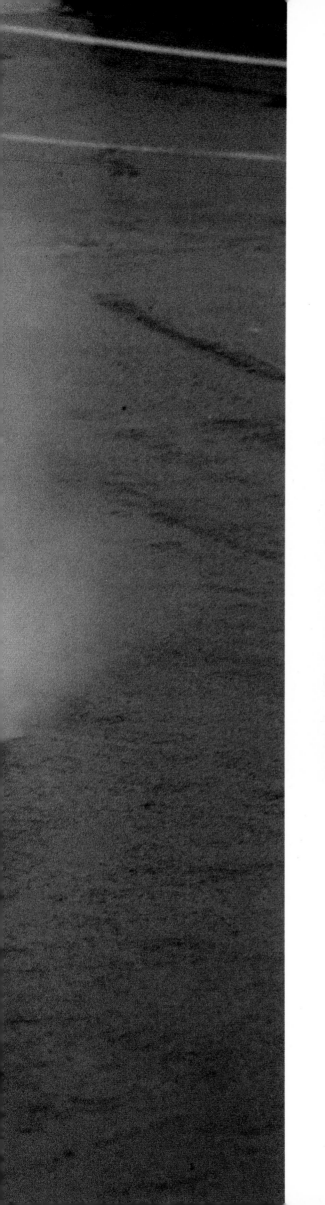

Frontal view of the Rial Arc 02- Cosworth, on board Christian Danner.

After his performance on the difficult Spa-Francorchamps track, Ayrton Senna da
Silva was proclaimed the undisputed "King of the Rain". This formidable driver
*seems to be at his acrobatic best on a wet track. Faster than anyone else, he
seems to love exceeding "safe" limits. Actually, his talents permit him to just about do
the impossible.*

The big disappointment of 1989 was the Ford engine that was specially prepared for the Benetton. In fact, it was clearly less powerful than the Honda, Ferrari and Renault. It was also not as reliable.

Here, frame by frame, we see the crazy, hair-raising take-off at the Grand Prix of France. By some fantastic miracle, the accident catalyzed by Mauricio Gugelmin didn't turn into a horrible tragedy. The slammed-on brakes raise clouds of smoke. The vehicles then touch wheels, and the scene on the track becomes a blood-curdling nightmare.

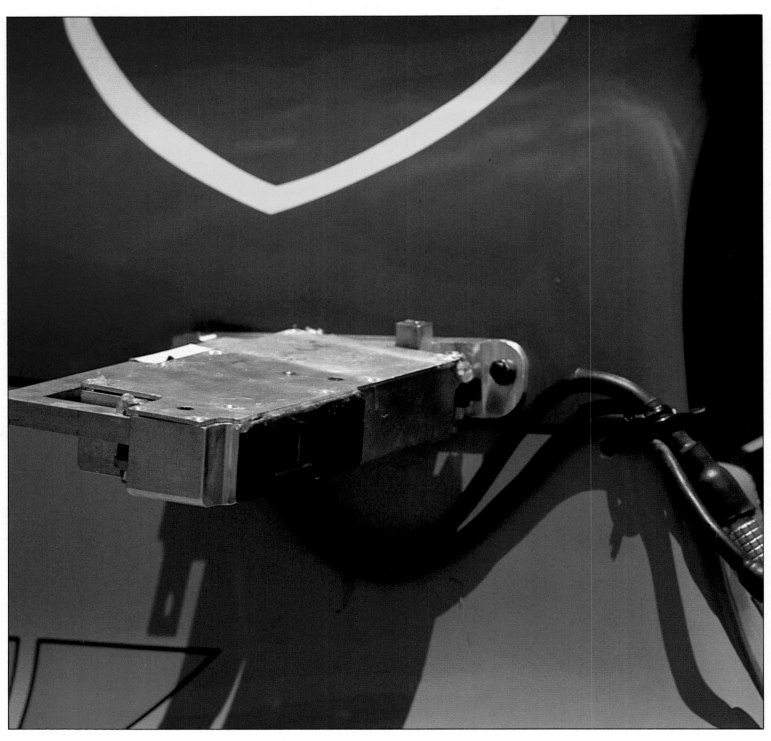

This telecamera provides emotion and tension to the viewing world. Each race a different team provides the images.

The callibration of the wheels, one of the most delicate of operations.

Eddie Cheever has run his last Formula 1 season. He has made a deal to drive for Jaguar in the World
Prototype events next season. He got tired of the poor competitiveness of the Arrows and having to struggle like mad
just to win a place in the last row of the starting grid.

(following page)

The season that just closed finally saw the debut of Mauro Forghieri's long-awaited 12-cylinder Lamborghini engine, which was fitted in a Lola-Larousse. This classic engine had lots of power but turned out to be rather unreliable.

Ayrton Senna leading the multicolored pack right after the start. He's already ahead of Nigel Mansell in his Ferrari by a few meters. The Brazilian ace always manages to take the pole position, and never fails to squeeze the maximum advantage out of it. He's the kind of guy that much rather prefers being the "hare" than the "hound".

The monumental Monte Carlo casino and its beautifully manicured gardens provide the charming setting for one of this city track's most famous curves: the Lowes.

Seeing the Monaco Grand Prix from one of the very expensive rooms in the Hotel Lowes is a genuine privilege. This is
a long-standing privilege that many traditionally enjoy by taking rooms in the luxury hotels overlooking the track.
(following page)

Nelson Piquet and Ayrton Senna "dancing in the rain." These two Brazilians have been bitter rivals right from the start. While at first the three-time world champion just watched condescendingly as the young "whippersnapper" from Sao Paolo started making a name for himself, he later made derisive and serious accusations regarding Senna's successes.

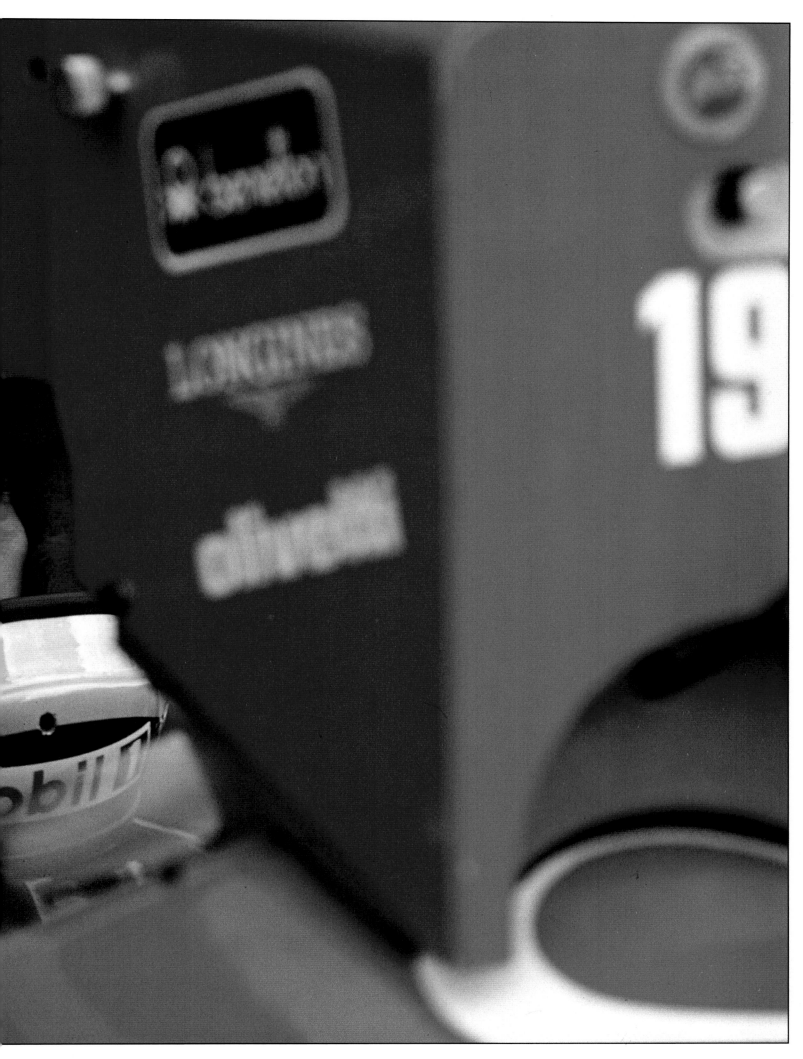

The man intently watching the trials on the service monitor is Alessandro Nannini, a very popular and outstanding driver from Siena, whose sister Gianna - a rock star - has also done quite well for herself.

The control check tag of the Ferrari number 27 driven by Mansell at the Monte Carlo Grand Prix held at the Principality, May 3, 1989.

It's a very familiar scene by now: the beautiful yachts anchored in the charming harbor, the stands and terraces teeming with excited fans, and the winding snake-like series of single-seaters making their pre-start warm-up lap of the track. Of course, it's the Monte Carlo Grand Prix shortly before the line-up and the green light: "the moment of truth".

(following page)

Satoru Nakajima moved into the Formula 1 in 1987, when Honda had this written in its contract with the two Lotus companies. Up to now, he's been best noted for his curiosity value.

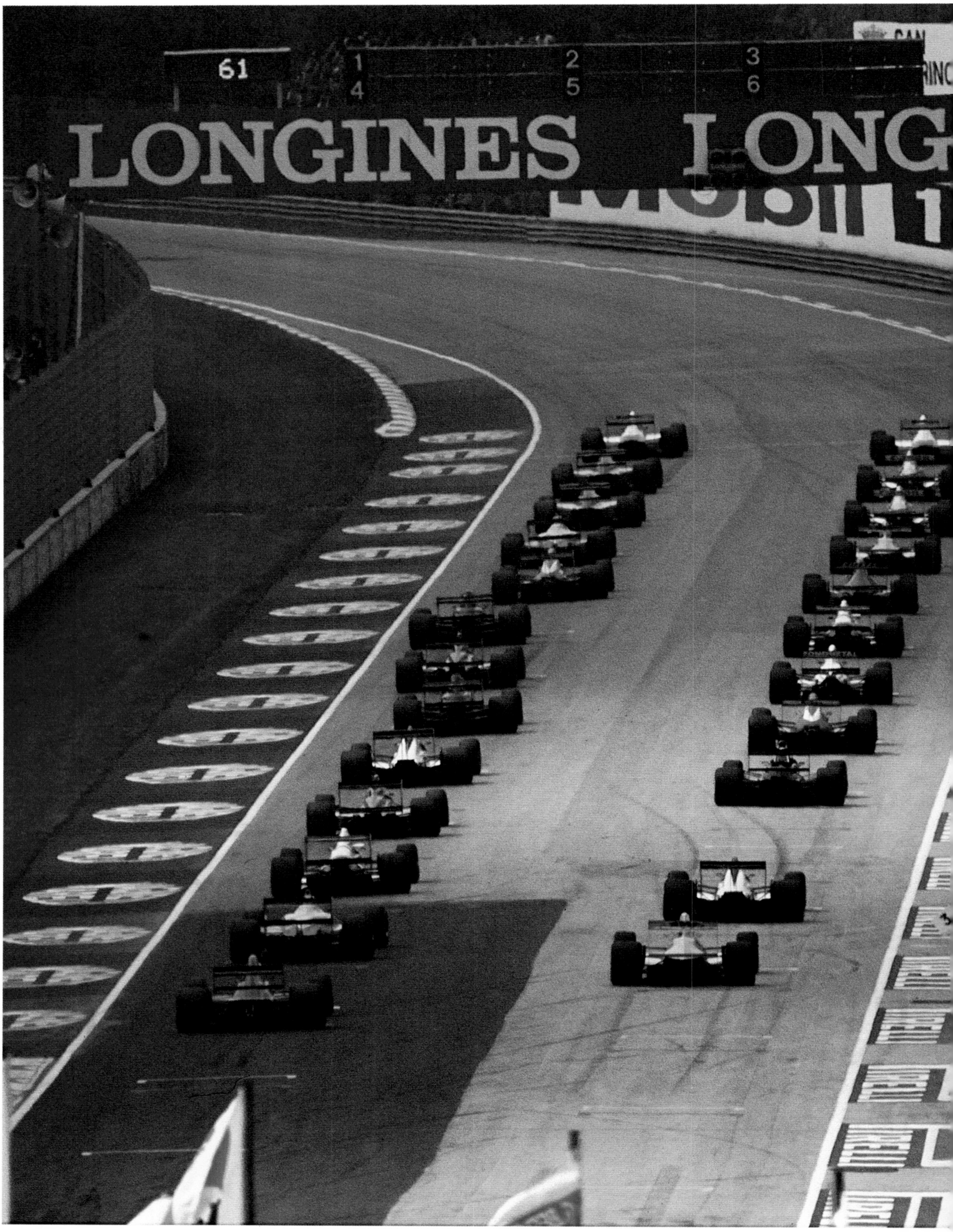
61
1 2 3
4 5 6
LONGINES

Here at Imola the telescopic lens condenses the start into one single roaring mass of machines and wheels. As when the bull charges out into the ring, this is also what is called "the moment of truth". All the highly-charged emotions of the drivers, pit men and the public are concentrated in this bolting ball of fury.

Larini in action, while centering his rear view mirror.

According to statistics, Ayrton Senna Da Silva is the fastest Formula 1 driver of all time. In the 1989 season, he even broke Jim Clark's record which, before this Brazilian decided to make the scene, was supposedly as solid as a rock.

Nigel Mansell in his Ferrari No. 27 is literally sending off sparks. No other photo could probably be so fraught with significance as this one, inasmuch as Mansell happens to be one of the most tigering drivers in the F1 environment.

Philippe Alliot concentrated on the wheel of his Lola LC-89.
(*preceding page*)
Alboreto, one of his sad returns to the pits while holding his personalized seat.

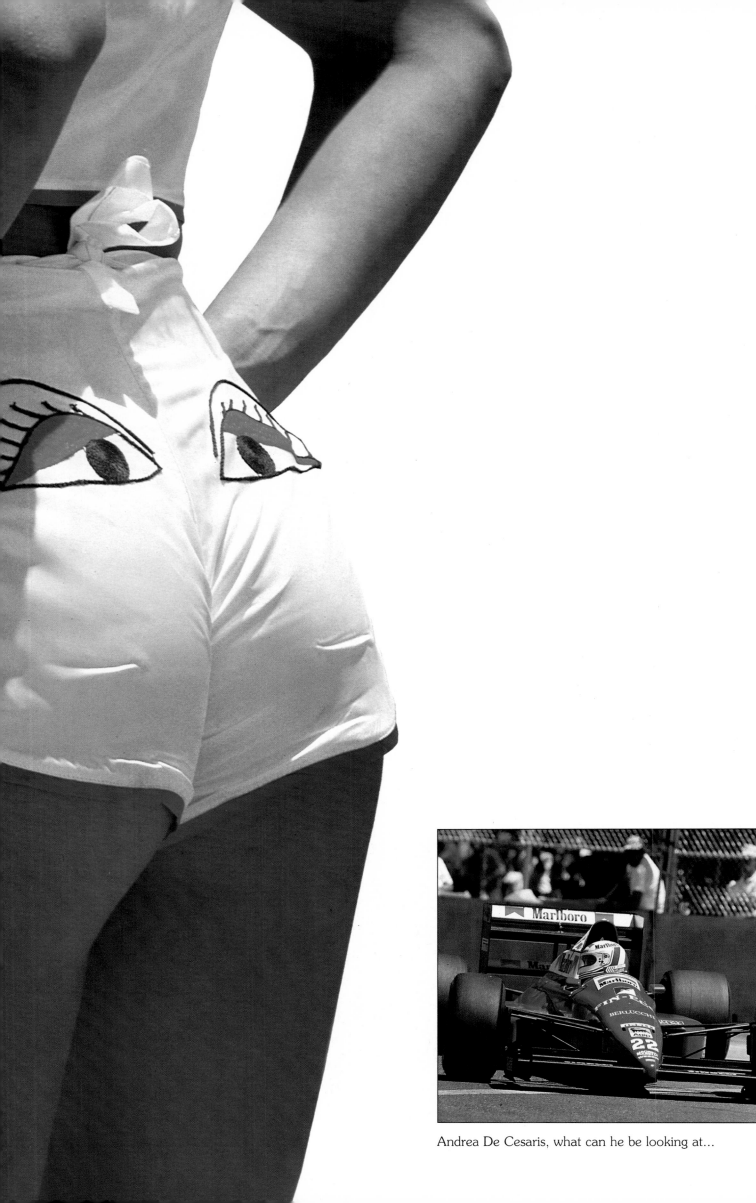

Andrea De Cesaris, what can he be looking at...

From the eyes of the pilot, immeasurable tension at the start line.

Three glances off track.

The really first-rate Hockenheim racetrack facilities, located near Heidelberg, have proved to be strongly competitive and have drawn the German Grand Prix event away from the new, featureless Nurburgring track. All of the Hockenhiem's 90,000 grandstand seats are numbered (with a large part of them under cover) and provide a spectacular view of the track.
(following page)

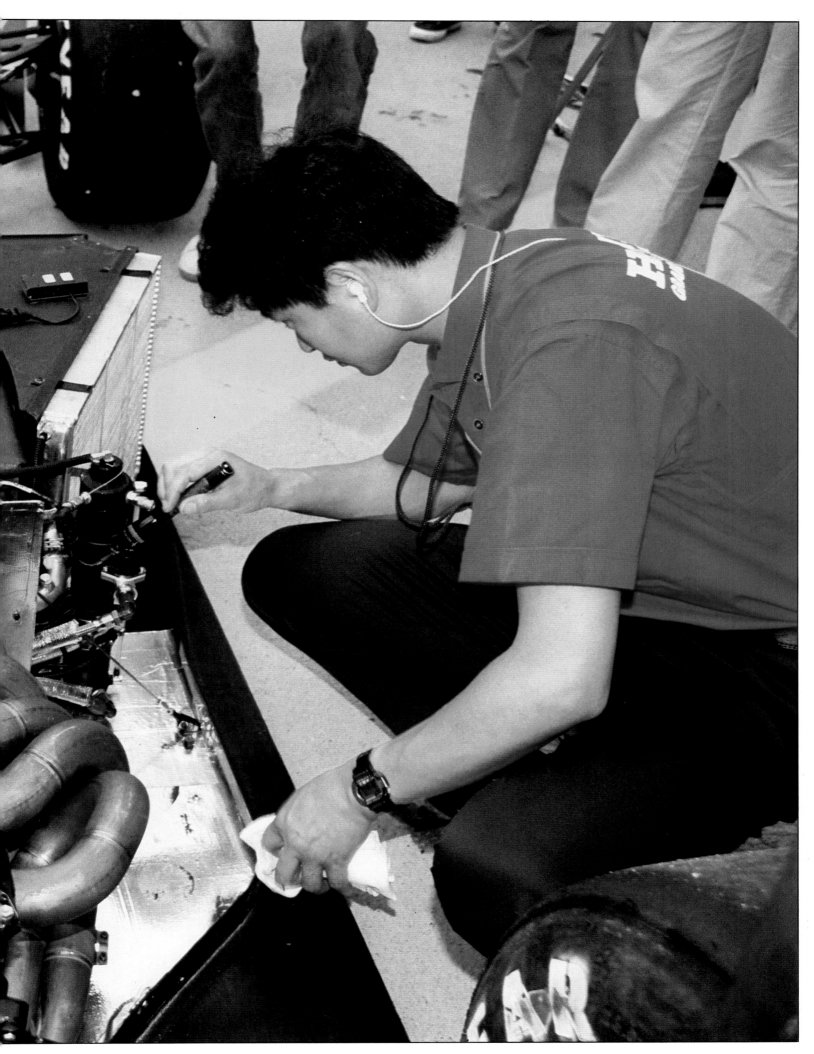

Honda's Formula 1 success is due to their research, organization, and strong financial position. But most of all, its success is due to the meticulousness of its mechanics, all of whom are graduate engineers. They apply themselves as religiously as if the future of their country depended on the outcome of the races.

When the Grand Prix racing tensions have calmed down and the prizes are handed out, our speed heros revert to what
they really are: young kids eager to celebrate their victories, like Ayrton Senna and Alessandro Nannini, here,
impatiently wrestling with the corks on their champagne magnums.

It's been a tradition now for several years that the day before the Canadian Grand Prix all the mechanics have a regata on the nearby river, using parts of Formula 1 cars as boats.

Not all the "racing" is done behind the wheel. A lot is done on foot to get across the track, to save precious time during the official trials, and sometimes to keep from getting soaked.

By this photo one wouldn't have been able to tell that this was to be Patrese's best year. In fact, he placed third in the World Championship classification behind Prost and Senna.

*World Champion
F1 '89*

G.P. BRASILE

R. Patrese
Williams
1'26"172
(210,180)

T. Boutsen
Williams
1'26"459
(209,482)

N. Mansell
Ferrari
1'26"772
(208,726)

D. Warwick
Arrows
1'27"408
(207,208)

J. Herbert
Benetton
1'27"626
(206,692)

M. Gugelmin
March
1'27"956
(205,917)

S. Modena
Brabham
1'28"621
(204,371)

P.L. Martini
Minardi
1'29"435
(202,511)

J. Palmer
Tyrrell
1'29"573
(202,199)

M. Alboreto
Tyrrell
1'30"255
(200,671)

O. Grouillard
Ligier
1'30"410
(200,327)

E. Cheever
Arrows
1'30"657
(199,782)

P. Alliot
Lola
1'31"009
(199,009)

A. Senna
Mc Laren
1'25"302
(212,323)

G. Berger
Ferrari
1'26"271
(209,938)

A. Prost
Mc Laren
1'26"620
(209,093)

I. Capelli
March
1'27"035
(208,096)

N. Piquet
Lotus
1'27"437
(207,139)

A. Nannini
Benetton
1'27"865
(206,130)

M. Brundle
Brabham
1'28"274
(205,175)

A. De Cesaris
BMS Dallara
1'29"005
(203,490)

C. Danner
Rial Arc
1'29"455
(202,466)

N. Larini
Osella
1'30"146
(200,914)

S. Nakajima
Lotus
1'30"375
(200,405)

L. Perez Sala
Minardi
1'30"643
(199,812)

B. Schneider
Zakspeed
1'30"861
(199,333)

26th of March, 1989. Now that all the winter trials were over, the testing of the new chassis, the evolution of the engines, and so on, the big crucial moment had arrived with all the cars out on the track, all together. It was the start of the start of the new Formula 1 championship. Yes, the new F1 championship because the rules had been changed. While for years the turbos had been permitted only a certain maximum amount of pressure thus limiting the amount of developed horsepower, they were now banned altogether. Now it's 3500 cc engines, a maximum of 12 cylinders, and no fuel limit.

What we were looking forward to knowing was if the McLaren-Honda that Senna drove to victory 15 out of 16 times in 1988, was also going to be the star of this new season?

Could it be that the John Barnard version of the Ferrari, with its electronically-managed transmission, was going to represent the McLaren's most perfect adversary?

Then, we were also waiting to know how the team qualifying would come out and who would be in the first 26 lucky point-earning positions.

The race at Rio, although being considered rather insignifi-cant with respect to the rest of the season, curiously gave some unexpected and contradictory results. For example, it was quite unexpected to see Nigel Mansell win in his maiden run with Ferrari and in a Ferrari which was also making its debut.

Then there was the McLaren that did so well in testing but

then ran into difficulty during the race, with Senna being put out of the race right off the bat after a tangle with Berger at the start, and later - half-way through the race - Prost limping along with only about half a clutch.

Mansell had had all kinds of trouble during testing. His transmission kept breaking down. At the warm-up before the race, he had pulled over after only a lap and a half because of the same old trouble, the transmission. But at the start of the race itself he took off like a bomb.

Poor Prost - with his ailing clutch which also kept him from making a tire change during the last part of the race - found himself having to eat Mansell's dust who had no trouble being first across the finish line to the delirious exultation of the spectators!

The surprising thing about all of this is that Mansell, at the half-way point, had to stop and have his tires changed, as well as his steering wheel, because the electronic gear-shifting equipment installed in it wasn't working properly.

Barnard himself hammered the new steering wheel down into place with his fists.

Gugelmin in his March made a great showing on his own home territory by taking 3rd place, which gave this English team (owned by Leyton House, a Japanese firm) a lot of hope for the future.

The strenuous race there at Rio was aggravated by the annoying heat, as usual. Another disconcerting outcome of this race was the Benetton's 4th place with Herbert at the wheel.

To put it briefly, the 1989 Grand Prix of Brazil for me was much more than the first race of the world championship. The importance of this race was actually multiplied because I was debuting in a Ferrari after a long string of winter tests.

I had such a difficult time with this car during testing and even afterwards, but for some miraculous reason the car ran just like clockwork from start to finish in this grueling race, and this is why I cut the finish ahead of the others.

At the end of this race I was really bushed, and if I hadn't trained so well during the winter, I don't think I'd have been able to make it. That extra stamina was also put to the test on that podium when I got myself a slashed hand on a sharp corner of the winner's trophy. But I was so happy I really didn't mind, and I also didn't even realize it was Easter... just about the best Easter I've ever had during my whole career.

Nigel Mansell

Rio, the first 1989 event and the first pleasant Ferrari surprise.

Two typical aspects of Rio: one worth appreciating, the other worth doing something about.

"Marco, get that contract signed with Mansell." This is what Enzo Ferrari ordered Piccinini. By mid-July he had accomplished his mission; the contract between Ferrari and Mansell was signed. In 1987 Michele Alboreto also signed with the team. Then there was Mansell's sensational backtracking and wanting out on the contract. With the world's title at stake and behind the wheel of the Williams Honda, the uncautious Nigel was afraid he was going to be boycotted by his team to the full advantage of his teammate and rival Nelson Piquet.

Intimidated by pressure brought to bear by the Williams clan - as well as unwise advice - Mansell went back to Maranello and tore up his contract. Neither Enzo Ferrari nor Marco Piccinini ever expected he'd ever go so far as to do that. Ferrari filed suit, but Mansell settled out of court and paid a very heavy penalty, which the Emilian patriarch promptly turned over to his favorite charity.

That seemed to be the end of Nigel Mansell's chances of ever racing for Ferrari again. But new things were happening. In June, Fiat - in a silent coup d'etat - absorbed Ferrari's racing car faction and set up a new policy. The new head man and general boss at Maranello was Vittorio Ghidella and the first thing he did was hire Nigel Mansell for the next season.

So, while Enzo Ferrari had put his foot down about even vaguely considering Nigel's return to Maranello - because he wasn't really unable to digest the kind of treatment he had gotten form Nigel in the summer of 1986 - there was Nigel back on the Ferrari team.

But some fans weren't all that enthusiastic about his return because he had replaced the Italian driver, Michele Alboreto. What also irked them a bit was the fact that Nigel was certainly no kid anymore and had had a rather inconsistent career.

For several years, good ol' Nigel had been Elio De Angelis' unimposing teammate with Lotus. He was such a nice fellow that they nicknamed him "the docile one". But when he went to work for Williams in 1985, he became a veritable Mr. Hyde. He lost all of his timidness and became a regular tiger on the track. In fact, he almost won the world title in 1986 and 1987. Well, all it took Nigel to win the enthusiastic acclaim of the Ferrari fans was a little less than an hour and a half: the time necessary to run the Brazilian Grand Prix. This was the first event of the 1989 championship series, and the one in which Nigel copped an altogether unexpected victory. Thus, a new love affair was born in Rio de Janeiro, a love affair between a tempestuous driver and passionate throng of Ferrari fans.

FINISHING ORDER

	DRIVER	CAR	AVERAGE	DELAY
1.	Nigel Mansell	Ferrari	186.034	
2.	Alain Prost	McLaren	185.790	7"809
3.	Mauricio Gugelmin	March	185.741	9"370
4.	Johnny Herbert	Benetton	185.706	10"493
5.	Derek Warwick	Arrows	185.476	17"866
6.	Alessandro Nannini	Benetton	185.464	18"241
7.	Jonathan Palmer	Tyrrell	181.168	1 lap
8.	Satoru Nakajima	Lotus	180.586	1 lap
9.	Olivier Grouillard	Ligier	179.955	1 lap
10.	Michele Alboreto	Tyrrell	178.288	2 laps
11.	Ayrton Senna	McLaren	177.439	2 laps
12.	Philippe Alliot	Lola	175.139	3 laps
13.	Andrea De Cesaris	Bms Dallara	182.701	4 laps
14.	Christian Danner	Rial Arc	171.118	5 laps

BEST LAPS

DRIVER AND CAR	LAP	TIME	AVERAGE
Patrese (Williams)	47	1'32"507	195.786
Nannini (Benetton)	42	1'33"361	193.995
Senna (McLaren)	55	1'33"685	193.324
Warwick (Arrows)	41	1'33"699	193.296
Mansell (Ferrari)	57	1'33"948	192.783
Herbert (Benetton)	45	1'34"164	192.341
Capelli (March)	18	1'34"479	191.700
Brundle (Brabham)	26	1'35"286	190.076
Palmer (Tyrrell)	43	1'35"327	189.994
Prost (McLaren)	17	1'35"341	189.967
De Cesaris (Bms Dallara)	40	1'35"402	189.845
Boutsen (Williams)	7	1'35"696	189.262
Gugelmin (March)	46	1'35"774	189.108
Grouillard (Ligier)	46	1'35"807	189.043
Nakajima (Lotus)	41	1'36"032	188.600
Danner (Rial Arc)	43	1'36"100	188.466
Cheever (Arrows)	22	1'36"394	187.891
Alboreto (Tyrrell)	58	1'36"747	187.206
Modena (Brabham)	7	1'37"470	185.817
Piquet (Lotus)	3	1'37"665	185.446
Schneider (Zakspeed)	20	1'37"789	185.211
Larini (Osella)	5	1'38"682	183.535
Alliot (Lola)	41	1'38"740	183.427
Martini (Minardi)	2	1'46"060	170.767

RETIREMENTS

DRIVER	CAR	LAPS	REASON
Gerhard Berger	Ferrari	0	Accident
Luis Perez Sala	Minardi	0	Accident
Pier Luigi Martini	Minardi	2	Engine bracket
Thierry Boutsen	Williams	3	Engine
Stefano Modena	Brabham	9	Half-shaft
Nicola Larini	Osella	10	Disqualified
Nelson Piquet	Lotus	10	Differential
Ivan Capelli	March	22	Suspension
Martin Brundle	Brabham	27	Engine
Bernd Schneider	Zakspeed Zk189	36	Accident
Eddie Cheever	Arrows	37	Accident
Riccardo Patrese	Williams	51	Alternator

G.P. SAN MARINO

A. Prost
Mc Laren
1'26"235
(210,402)

R. Patrese
Williams
1'27"920
(206,369)

T. Boutsen
Williams
1'28"308
(205,463)

N. Piquet
Lotus
1'29"057
(203,735)

O. Grouillard
Ligier
1'29"104
(203,627)

D. Warwick
Arrows
1'29"281
(203,224)

N. Larini
Osella
1'29"488
(202,753)

A. De Cesaris
Bms Dallara
1'29"669
(202,344)

G. Tarquini
Ags
1'29"913
(201,795)

P. Alliot
Lola
1'30"168
(201,224)

M. Brundle
Brabham
1'30"271
(200,995)

S. Nakajima
Lotus
1'30"697
(200,051)

Y. Dalmas
Lola
1'31"137
(199,085)

A. Senna
Mc Laren
1'26"010
(210,952)

N. Mansell
Ferrari
1'27"652
(207,000)

G. Berger
Ferrari
1'28"089
(205,974)

A. Nannini
Benetton
1'28"854
(204,200)

A. Caffi
Bms Dallara
1'29"069
(203,707)

P. Martini
Minardi
1'29"152
(203,518)

I. Capelli
March
1'29"385
(202,987)

L. Perez Sala
Minardi
1'29"503
(202,719)

S. Modena
Brabham
1'29"761
(202,137)

M. Gugelmin
March
1'30"163
(201,236)

E. Cheever
Arrows
1'30"233
(201,079)

J. Herbert
Benetton
1'30"347
(200,826)

J. Palmer
Tyrrell
1'30"928
(199,542)

Not even a month had past from the Brazilian event and we were already eagerly awaiting the results of this next race. The Brazilian results weren't having any influence on what the forecasters were saying. Imola, a fast track, has lots of hills and dales and wide, medium-fast curves, which is right down Senna's alley. He proved it all the way but with his teammate Prost right behind him.

There was a little rivalry going on at Ferrari between Gerhard Berger and Nigel Mansell. It seemed that Gerhard was a bit miffed about his teammate's luck. He was actually chaffing over the fact that - as usually happens - Mansell, the newcomer with his beginner's luck, had everybody at Ferrari going ga-ga over him and giving him the "fair-haired boy" treatment. Gerhard also noticed that the fans had changed their focus of interest. For Ferrari, Imola is the best indicator for anything of this sort.

So, while over at McLaren's there was the friction between Senna and Prost, Ferrari was having the same problems with Berger and Mansell, although Ferrari's problems were compounded by Barnard, whose future with Ferrari was beginning to look a little doubtful.

The Imola race actually answered a few questions. While the McLaren double-header was, of course, an achievement of considerable note, the real highlight of this race was Berger's dramatic accident which happened on the second lap. He was going just under 300 km/h while taking the curve past the pits when he lost part of his front spoiler. It jammed into his wheels and made him lose control.

Off he went towards the TV cameras and crunched into the side protective wall. There was a big burst of flame as the spilt fuel immediately ignited and he was trapped in there, knocked out and being slowly barbecued.

The rescue crews were on the spot in just a few seconds and they had the fire out, and him too, in almost less time than it takes to tell about it. Incredibly Berger was only just a little stunned and had a few slight superficial burns. Everybody who saw the accident would have sworn he'd had had it. It was absolutely incredible how he came out of that terrible accident with such relatively little bodily damage.

All of this speaks exceedingly well for both the cockpit design, drivers' protective clothing, and, of course, the superb crash emergency crews and the excellence of their training. The high-strength carbon-fiber composites used in the body design efficiently absorbs quite a bit of the direct impact, leaving only a minor part of it to be transmitted to the driver.

Mansell in his Ferrari had to step back into the ranks after his transmission trouble retired him. The trouble wasn't whipped until after the first part of this season was over. He had to suffer through both the tests and the race itself. With the track still wet Berger's best time on Friday wasn't good enough and this turned out to be pretty costly because that gave Nannini his victory and allowed the old Benetton with its 1988 engine also to place. Benetton's getting its new F1 engine just as soon as its ready. Palmer's 5th in his debuting Tyrrell was noteworthy. Albroreto didn't do so well in practice; he didn't qualify and Palmer took advantage of the situation.

This is the track I like the best. It's just perfect for me, both as regards environment and speed.

My five years with Minardi, which is at Faenza about 10 kilometers from Imola, is full of wonderful memories, especially of that great place even though it's generally a Ferrari place.

However, I still feel very much at home here and get all charged up when I race here. This is probably why I can always be sure of being able to do my very best.

The "Enzo and Dino Ferrari" is great. You have fast acceleration and braking places, then slow curves, real wide curves, chicanes, more curves and then more fast acceleration and braking stretches, and you can pick up 5-7 tenths on each of these over those who aren't used to this type of track.

I'm always happy when I'm scheduled to race on this track.

Alessandro Nannini

His honor, Mr. Gava, the Minister of the Interior, presides at the inauguration of the Imola track and its dedication to the memory of Enzo and Dino Ferrari.

it is today. It was Enzo's appropriate strategy suggestions that permitted the successful overcoming of the considerable number of obstacles that threatened to impede realization. It wasn't until 1979 that the Imola track finally became a full-fledged "autodrome", at which time it was appropriately named after Enzo Ferrari's son Dino, who died while still a young man.

With Enzo Ferrari's death in August of 1988, it seemed logical to the Automobile Club of Bologna and Sagis - the company that manages the track - that this particular San Marino Grand Prix event was the right occasion for putting Enzo's together with Dino's as the name of the track.

The unveiling of the marble slab at the track entrance was quite an informal affair with a touch of festivity. Besides the Minister of the Interior, Mr. Gava, there was also Jean Marie Balestre, the President of FISA, and Fabrizio Serena, the President of CSAI. The photograph also shows Pietro Lardi Ferrari, who, being a rather self-effacing person, perfers to stay out of the spotlight.

With a few heartfelt words, Pietro remembered his father and how much he had always been sentimentally attached to the Imola track. In the background we have the almost symbolic presence of two Ferrari drivers: Nigel Mansell and Gerhard Berger.

The photo we choose here to remember the 1989 San Marino Grand Prix is really quite symbolic, because it represents Italian sports history, the Italian passion for racing cars and all the magic evoked by the name Ferrari.

We call this track the little Nurburgring. The Imola track was once only a semi-permanent track installation without a very secure future. Its rolling hills, however, seemed to provide just what the drivers and public wanted in the way of spectacular racing.

It was the unswerving determination on the part of a group of strong-willed men that made it possible to transform it into a highly popular track. Had it not been for Enzo Ferrari, it would probably never have become the famous track

This 1989 San Marino Grand Prix shot is truly representative or Italian sports history, beginning with the post-war years, and reflects the Italian's passion for engines and all the facination evoked by the name Ferrari.

It was rapid intervenetion of this ambulance that saved Gerhard Berger's life.

FINISHING ORDER

	DRIVER	CAR	AVERAGE	DELAY
1.	**Ayrton Senna**	McLaren	201.939	
2.	**Alain Prost**	McLaren	200.392	40"225
3.	**Alessandro Nannini**	Benetton	197.879	1 lap
4.	**Derek Warwick**	Arrows	196.008	1 lap
5.	**Jonathan Palmer**	Tyrrell	195.284	1 lap
6.	**Gabriele Tarquini**	Ags	195.038	1 lap
7.	**Eddie Cheever**	Arrows	193.147	2 laps
8.	**Andrea De Cesaris**	Bms Dallara	192.837	2 laps
9.	**Johnny Herbert**	Benetton	190.968	2 laps
10.	**Nicola Larini**	Osella	193.693	6 laps

BEST LAPS

DRIVER AND CAR	LAP	TIME	AVERAGE
Prost (McLaren)	45	1'26"795	209.044
Senna (McLaren)	37	1'27"273	207.899
Mansell (Ferrari)	18	1'29"849	201.939
Nannini (Benetton)	49	1'29"868	201.896
Patrese (Williams)	13	1'29"959	201.692
De Cesaris (Bms Dallara)	52	1'29"995	201.611
Palmer (Tyrrell)	49	1'30"164	201.233
Tarquini (Ags)	53	1'30"364	200.788
Cheever (Arrows)	30	1'30"728	199.982
Warwick (Arrows)	36	1'30"749	199.936
Piquet (Lotus)	28	1'30"771	199.888
Herbert (Benetton)	50	1'31"020	199.341
Larini (Osella)	15	1'31"791	197.666
Sala (Minardi)	38	1'31"948	197.329
Nakajima (Lotus)	43	1'31"970	197.282
Gugelmin (March)	16	1'32"038	197.136
Brundle (Brabham)	27	1'32"189	196.813
Modena (Brabham)	18	1'32"618	195.901
Berger (Ferrari)	3	1'33"319	194.430
Martini (Minardi)	5	1'34"525	191.949
Capelli (March)	1	1'42"912	176.306

RETIREMENTS

DRIVER	CAR	LAPS	REASON
Yannick Dalmas	Lola	0	No start
Alex Caffi	Bms Dallara	0	Disqualified
Thierry Boutsen	Williams	0	Disqualified
Olivier Grouillard	Ligier	0	Disqualified
Philippe Alliot	Lola	0	Engine
Ivan Capelli	March	1	Accident
Gerhard Berger	Ferrari	3	Accident
Pier Luigi Martini	Minardi	6	Gearbox
Stefano Modena	Brabham	19	Accident
Riccardo Patrese	Williams	21	Engine
Nigel Mansell	Ferrari	23	Gearbox
Nelson Piquet	Lotus	29	Engine
Mauricio Gugelmin	March	39	Gearbox
Luis Perez Sala	Minardi	43	Accident
Satoru Nakajima	Lotus	46	Battery
Martin Brundle	Brabham	51	Fuel pump

G.P. MONACO

A. Prost
Mc Laren
1'22"456
(145,299)

M. Brundle
Brabham
1'24"580
(141,650)

D. Warwick
Arrows
1'24"791
(141,298)

S. Modena
Brabham
1'25"086
(140,808)

A. De Cesaris
Bms Dallara
1'25"515
(140,102)

M. Alboreto
Tyrrell
1'26"388
(138,686)

M. Gugelmin
March
1'26"522
(138,471)

O. Grouillard
Ligier
1'26"792
(138,040)

P.H. Raphanel
Coloni
1'27"011
(137,693)

E. Cheever
Arrows
1'27"117
(137,525)

I. Capelli
March
1'27"302
(137,234)

J. Herbert
Benetton
1'27"706
(136,602)

L. Perez Sala
Minardi
1'27"786
(136,477)

A. Senna
Mc Laren
1'22"308
(145,561)

T. Boutsen
Williams
1'24"332
(142,067)

N. Mansell
Ferrari
1'24"735
(141,391)

R. Patrese
Williams
1'25"021
(140,916)

A. Caffi
Bms Dallara
1'25"481
(140,157)

P.L. Martini
Minardi
1'26"288
(138,847)

G. Tarquini
Ags
1'26"422
(138,631)

A. Nannini
Benetton
1'26"599
(138,348)

P. Alliot
Lola
1'26"857
(137,937)

N. Piquet
Lotus
1'27"046
(137,638)

R. Arnoux
Ligier
1'27"182
(137,423)

J. Palmer
Tyrrell
1'27"452
(136,999)

R. Moreno
Coloni
1'27"721
(136,578)

Yes, this is the third Italian world championship race, what with the fans, flags, enthusiasm, and Monaco's closeness to the Italian way of life. When a Ferrari gets out on that track, it's like being home.

But there was only one Ferrari at this race, with Mansell driving. Berger was still convalescing, not so much physically as psychologically.

He was feeling very well and was on the scene both to watch the race and comment on the Austrian TV. The deep burn in his right hand was healing O.K., but more time will be needed to heal completely. Mansell (probably because he had his mind on 1990), but he was the one who finally found out what the technical problem was that had caused Berger's accident at Imola.

The Ferrari nose and front wings stand up very well to aerodynamic forces coming from above, but the connections are not strong enough to withstand loads from below. The curbs on the curves are high enough to permit the Ferrari's side wings up front to easily contact them, thus putting a large stress on the connection points.

So, what happened at Imola was that the high aerodynamic loads coming from below put too much of a strain on the joints and caused the loss of the nose and wings.

Barnard solved this problem by putting softer strips along the sides and beefing up the nose and front-wing attachments. But this didn't help bring the two McLarens within reach. Senna - who certainly hadn't forgotten how his lack of concentration in 1988 had caused him to run into the guard rail (when he was ahead by a full minute!) - was very, very careful this time and racked up his second straight win, while Prost had to be content with his third straight 2nd place.

The Brazilian performed like a Swiss watch. He was exceptionally fast in the time trials, and managed his prowess during the race with superior effectiveness and determination. The Ferrari's electronically-controlled transmission not only gave problems during the time trials but caused the car to drop out of the race.

As is traditional with each Monte Carlo race, there's always some outsider who makes a surprisingly good showing. And this time it was Stefano Modena, who reaped a heap of glory for himself as he stood up there on the podium with Senna and Prost.

His fans were especially enthusiastic about him, not only for this exceptional performance, but also because of his modest, retiring manner (at least in the pits).

The Scuderia Italia was also celebrating because of Caffi's 4th place and De Cesaris' great performance.

I love Monte Carlo for a whole lot of reasons. First of all, I love it because this is where I won my first F1 Grand Prix. Then I love it because this is where I live and work. Furthermore, I love the great atmosphere you have here when the Grand Prix is on. It's uniqu; you won't find anything else like it anywhere in the world. It's a street circuit with authentic curves: the Casino, the Tunnel, the Tobacco Shop, and the Pool chicane. It's actually a real track even though it's been defined as "the classical street circuit." Another reason why I'm so fond of this track is because the day I won my first Grand Prix was the last time Grace Kelly appeared on the podium.

Riccardo Patrese

anxiously waiting right from the early morning hours. The usual program included a long stop at the Ferrari pit, where he would exchange a few words with each and every person there, would give a few words of encouragement to the drivers and then go make a quick visit to the other pits.

The visit would wind up with a little press conference with some needling by the journalists and some snappy answers. For example, when asked what he thought about the Japanese, Mr. Agnelli quipped back, "It's a good thing they don't know how to play soccer." Gianni Agnelli must have been a little tired of the old routine because this year he pulled a surprise on everybody. He showed up without fanfare, late Friday afternoon which is the day the F1 drivers in Monte Carlo take a break; their test runs are on Thursday and Saturday. Mr. Agnelli showed up behind the wheel of a small motorboat and pulled up to the dock just long enough take a few friends aboard, such as Cesare Fiorio, Nigel Mansell and John Barnard, and then left with all those disappointed and dejected people, who had been waiting for him for such a long time, completely thunderstruck. The small boat headed straight for Mr. Agnelli's beautiful yacht - which was anchored a short distance offshore - where they sat down to tea out on the deck. The people back on terra firma who were the most disappointed were the Ferrari fans: kids in blue jeans, teenagers in tennis shoes, middle-aged gentlemen with all types of cameras, all from various parts of Italy.

A familiar figure at the Monte Carlo event, Mr. Agnelli - President of the Fiat Company, takes Cesare Fiorio and Nigel Mansell to where they can have a private chat, away from any inquisitive intruders.

Fascinating Monte Carlo

Mr. Agnelli was the guest everybody was anxiously waiting for, and his little walk through the pits was practically worth the price of the ticket. From time immemorial, Mr. Agnelli - Fiat's President - has always shown up on Saturdays, always accompanied by some friend and few discrete bodyguards. But this time no one knew just what time he would be showing up, which kept photographers and journalists

The "third Italian Grand Prix" event's three point-winning Italians: Alboreto in his new Tyrrell (without having run the Thursday trials); Modena who came in 3rd (thanks to the Pirelli tires); and Caffi, after having brilliantly made it through the pre-qualification runs.

FINISHING ORDER

	DRIVER	CAR	AVERAGE	DELAY
1.	**Ayrton Senna**	McLaren	135.401	
2.	**Alain Prost**	McLaren	134.365	52"529
3.	**Stefano Modena**	Brabham	133.336	1 lap
4.	**Alex Caffi**	Bms Dallara	131.876	2 laps
5.	**Michele Alboreto**	Tyrrell	131.376	2 laps
6.	**Martin Brundle**	Brabham	131.133	2 laps
7.	**Eddie Cheever**	Arrows	130.918	2 laps
8.	**Alessandro Nannini**	Benetton	129.968	3 laps
9.	**Jonathan Palmer**	Tyrrell	129.952	3 laps
10.	**Thierry Boutsen**	Williams	129.950	3 laps
11.	**Ivan Capelli**	March	131.295	4 laps
12.	**René Arnoux**	Ligier	128.234	4 laps
13.	**Andrea De Cesaris**	Bms Dallara	127.796	4 laps
14.	**Johnny Herbert**	Benetton	127.486	4 laps
15.	**Riccardo Patrese**	Williams	127.308	4 laps

RETIREMENTS

DRIVER	CAR	LAPS	REASON
Derek Warwick	Arrows	2	Electrical system
Pier Luigi Martini	Minardi	3	Half-shaft
Olivier Grouillard	Ligier	4	Gearbox
Pierre Henri Raphanel	Coloni	19	Gearbox
Nigel Mansell	Ferrari	30	Gearbox
Nelson Plquet	Lotus	32	Accident
Mauricio Gugelmin	March	36	Engine
Philippe Alliot	Lola	38	Engine
Roberto Moreno	Coloni	44	Gearbox
Gabriele Tarquini	Ags	46	Computer
Luis Perez Sala	Minardi	48	Engine

BEST LAPS

DRIVER AND CAR	LAP	TIME	AVERAGE
Prost (McLaren)	59	1'25"501	140.125
Brundle (Brabham)	58	1'25"882	139.503
Senna (McLaren)	23	1'26"017	139.284
Patrese (Williams)	66	1'26"369	138.716
Mansell (Ferrari)	29	1'26"946	137.796
De Cesaris (Bms Dallara)	71	1'27"240	137.331
Boutsen (Williams)	62	1'27"290	137.253
Palmer (Tyrrell)	70	1'27"745	136.541
Modena (Brabham)	73	1'28"188	135.855
Capelli (March)	71	1'28"204	135.831
Cheever (Arrows)	71	1'28"506	135.367
Caffi (Bms Dallara)	58	1'28"680	135.101
Alboreto (Tyrrell)	71	1'29"063	134.521
Tarquini (Ags)	32	1'29"203	134.309
Nannini (Benetton)	28	1'29"251	134.237
Alliot (Lola)	8	1'29"446	133.945
Herbert (Benetton)	43	1'29"685	133.588
Piquet (Lotus)	28	1'29"808	133.405
Sala (Minardi)	16	1'30"890	131.816
Moreno (Coloni)	31	1'31"114	131.492
Raphanel (Coloni)	15	1'31"253	131.292
Arnoux (Ligier)	15	1'31"358	131.141
Warwick (Arrows)	2	1'32"050	130.155
Martini (Minardi)	3	1'32"270	129.845
Gugelmin (March)	5	1'32"334	129.755
Grouillard (Ligier)	2	1'34"265	127.097

G.P. MESSICO

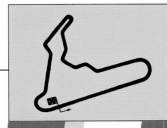

A. Prost
Mc Laren
1'18"773
(202,044)

I. Capelli
March
1'19"337
(200,608)

G. Berger
Ferrari
1'19"835
(199,356)

T. Boutsen
Williams
1'20"234
(198,365)

D. Warwick
Arrows
1'20"601
(197,462)

A. De Cesaris
Bms Dallara
1'20"873
(196,797)

A. Nannini
Benetton
1'20"888
(196,761)

P. Alliot
Lola
1'21"031
(196,414)

J. Herbert
Benetton
1'21"105
(196,235)

M. Brundle
Brabham
1'21"217
(195,964)

P.L. Martini
Minardi
1'21"471
(195,353)

E. Cheever
Arrows
1'21"716
(194,767)

N. Piquet
Lotus
1'21"831
(194,494)

A. Senna
Mc Laren
1'17"876
(204,371)

N. Mansell
Ferrari
1'19"137
(201,115)

R. Patrese
Williams
1'19"656
(199,804)

M. Alboreto
Tyrrell
1'20"066
(198,781)

S. Modena
Brabham
1'20"505
(197,697)

O. Grouillard
Ligier
1'20"859
(196,832)

J. Palmer
Tyrrell
1'20"888
(196,761)

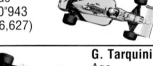
S. Nakajima
Lotus
1'20"943
(196,627)

G. Tarquini
Ags
1'21"031
(196,414)

A. Caffi
Bms Dallara
1'21"139
(196,152)

S. Johansson
Onyx
1'21"696
(195,624)

C. Danner
Rial
1'21"696
(194,815)

R. Arnoux
Ligier
1'21"830
(194,496)

The championship events were now really going at full steam, and no more time could be devoted to development. The races were being held weekly, and the car damage from the previous Grand Prix had to be repaired in time for the next.

This track at Mexico City is at 2000 meters of altitude, and this means thinner air and consequent loss of power, which varies between 25 and 30 percent. This time none of the engines were turbocharged, which put them all on an equal level.

The track had its same old problems of bumps, holes, roughness, and large, 5th gear, 180-degree turns at over 200 km/h.

The Ferrari people weren't sure if Berger was going to be all right in time for this race, also considering, of course, the difficulties involved with this track.

Cesare Fiorio had worked a deal with the Osella team whereby he could have Nicola Larini as a stand-in for Berger. Berger was already making noises to the effect that the Ferrari was not competitive and reliable enough for him. This, plus the fact that Fiorio had worked a deal with Osella, was almost convincing evidence for those in the know that Mansell's teammate for 1990 was going to be the young, promising driver from Tuscany.

Larini went through a lot of intensive, preparatory training for the job. He was especially eager to get used to the semi-automatic shift, keep his foot off the clutch, both hands on the wheel, and shift gears by moving his finger

behind the wheel.

But no driver - whatever his physical handicap - can resist the temptation of getting back behind the wheel, regardless of whether or not he's got pains or is missing a couple of pieces of skin, and this includes, of course, Berger. Though still not in top physical shape, he decided he wanted to race in the Mexican event. This left Larini with a kind of a sour taste in his mouth as he glumly went back to his Osella.

The time trials once again revealed that Aryton Senna has an insatiable appetite for pole positions and checkered flags. It was Senna's third straight victory, and it looked like he was on his way to win his second title for sure. If Senna doesn't have to contend with mechanical problems, he's just plain unbeatable, and this includes his teammate.

While there is a certain sense of satisfaction in the Ferrari camp, things are not quite the same in the McLaren-Honda camp where Prost and Senna are giving each other the cold shoulder. Prost keeps insisting that, at Imola, he and Senna had supposedly agreed to soft-pedal the belligerence during the first lap, but that Senna had just plain ignored the agreement and taken unfair advantage of the situation. So, Prost is looking for new pastures, new motivations; the McLaren can no longer provide them. If this is so, what about Senna?

This Mexican Grand Prix was won by Senna, with Riccardo Patrese coming in 2nd, which finally gave Renault its long-awaited satisfaction, and also increased its hope for a more promising future. The Renault, the same 1988 version, still hadn't fully met its expectations.

This is one of those tracks that I just can't like. It's the scenes that you've got at certain points along the track especially along the curve leading to the pits. I just can't digest it.

You have to train a long time before going to Mexico City. It's the elevation, the heat and the terrible smog. The worst drawback of all, of course, is Montezuma's revenge that relentlessly massacres the insides of a lot of unsuspecting foreign visitors. But after all, we really should remember that it's the Grand Prix of Mexico! Quoting from one of the songs written by my friend Vasco Rossi, "I'm going to Mexico and I'm letting out all the stops". I'm going to try to do the same, to improve my performance. Another characteristic of this track is its horrible paving job. It's got bumps, rough spots, holes; and you can easily imagine how much fun it is to barrel along that kind of a track with your teeth almost being knocked out of your head. Both man and machine take a rough beating, I can tell you, and it's no wonder that preformance levels are often disappointing.

For me this is the toughest Grand Prix of the whole season.

Alex Caffi

Gerhard Berger will make his reappearance on the racing scene at the Mexico City race track, the one named after the Rodriguez brothers. About a month has gone by since his accident at Imola where he came out of it practically intact. All he got out of that blood-chilling accident was a broken rib and a few superficial burns. When he went off the curve in his Ferrari on the that first turn on the Santerno track, hit the protecting wall and burst into flames, it looked like he would not arrive for sure. There was absolutely no way that he could have come out of that alive. Yet he did! It was nothing less than a bona fide miracle! He just spent a few days in a clinic at Innsbruck - he insisted on being taken back to his native Austria - and then went to Niki Lauda's very serious physiotherapist to get back into shape physically and mentally. He insisted on being present at Monte Carlo, not, of course, to race but just to keep in contact with the environment.

On Sunday he was the sportscaster for Austrian TV, at which time he announced that he was going to be ready to race in the Mexico City event. The Ferrari people, however, seemed to have another opinion since they asked to have Osella on loan for the Mexican race.

This young driver from Tuscany was even asked to go to Fiorano and do some test runs with the Ferrari to get used to the automatic shift. When Berger heard about this he reacted with decisiveness, also went to Fiorano and made some test runs, after which he said he was ready to go. The Ferrari people were practically obligated to let him have the No.28 for the Mexican Grand Prix, but their hesitancy was pretty blatant. It was quite obvious that they weren't so sure that Berger's accident at Imola hadn't left a permanent scar and that he would never again be the fast, intrepid driver of his pr-aaccident days.

And so it was at that particular time that Berger and Ferrari had a falling out, with Ferrari having the haunting feeling that they were letting a champion slip through their fingers, and Berger with his pride mortally wounded.

As Michele had already forecast - "I'll come in 3rd" - that's just what he did.

Willie Dugle, Lauda's physical therapist, did a good job on Berger, who only has to sit out one event: the Grand Prix of Monte Carlo.

FINISHING ORDER

	DRIVER	CAR	AVERAGE	DELAY
1.	**Ayrton Senna**	McLaren	191.941	
2.	**Riccardo Patrese**	Williams	191.420	15"560
3.	**Michele Alboreto**	Tyrrell	190.898	31"254
4.	**Alessandro Nannini**	Benetton	190.427	45"495
5.	**Alain Prost**	McLaren	190.077	56"113
6.	**Gabriele Tarquini**	Ags	189.041	1 lap
7.	**Eddie Cheever**	Arrows	188.750	1 lap
8.	**Olivier Grouillard**	Ligier	188.555	1 lap
9.	**Martin Brundle**	Brabham	188.460	1 lap
10.	**Stefano Modena**	Brabham	188.248	1 lap
11.	**Nelson Piquet**	Lotus	187.276	1 lap
12.	**Christian Danner**	Rial Arc	186.008	2 laps
13.	**Alex Caffi**	Bms Dallara	183.790	2 laps
14.	**René Arnoux**	Ligier	183.374	3 laps
15.	**Johnny Herbert**	Benetton	182.648	3 laps

BEST LAPS

DRIVER AND CAR	LAP	TIME	AVERAGE
Mansell (Ferrari)	41	1'20"420	197.906
Prost (McLaren)	43	1'20"506	197.695
Senna (McLaren)	43	1'20"585	197.501
Alboreto (Tyrrell)	43	1'21"230	195.933
Patrese (Williams)	42	1'21"383	195.564
Grouillard (Ligier)	63	1'22"093	193.873
Nannini (Benetton)	50	1'22"110	193.833
Cheever (Arrows)	54	1'22"111	193.830
Modena (Brabham)	41	1'22"233	193.543
Tarquini (Ags)	44	1'22"318	193.343
Brundle (Brabham)	52	1'22"344	193.282
Piquet (Lotus)	54	1'22"560	192.776
Alliot (Lola)	27	1'22"593	192.699
Warwick (Arrows)	32	1'22"777	192.271
Nakajima (Lotus)	34	1'22"907	191.969
Berger (Ferrari)	15	1'22"981	191.798
Boutsen (Williams)	15	1'22"991	191.775
Herbert (Benetton)	42	1'23"095	191.535
Johansson (Onyx)	14	1'23"416	190.798
Danner (Rial Arc)	52	1'23"524	190.551
Martini (Minardi)	48	1'23"539	190.517
Arnoux (Ligier)	43	1'23"867	189.772
Caffi (Bms Dallara)	30	1'24"527	188.890
Palmer (Tyrrell)	8	1'24"660	187.994
De Cesaris (Bms Dallara)	11	1'25"424	186.313

RETIREMENTS

DRIVER	CAR	LAPS	REASON
Ivan Capelli	March	0	Axle
Jonathan Palmer	Tyrrell	9	Accelerator
Thierry Boutsen	Williams	15	Electrical system
Stefan Johansson	Onyx	16	Transmission
Gerhard Berger	Ferrari	16	Gearbox
Andrea De Cesaris	Bms Dallara	20	Suspension system
Philippe Alliot	Lola	28	Electrical system
Satoru Nakajima	Lotus	35	Accident
Derek Warwick	Arrows	35	Electrical system
Nigel Mansell	Ferrari	43	Gearbox
Pier Luigi Martini	Minardi	53	Engine

G.P. STATI UNITI

A. Prost
Mc Laren
1'31"517
(149,480)

N. Mansell
Ferrari
1'31"927
(148,814)

A. Caffi
Bms Dallara
1'32"160
(148,438)

G. Berger
Ferrari
1'32"364
(148,110)

D. Warwick
Arrows
1'32"492
(147,905)

P. Alliot
Lola
1'32"562
(147,793)

R. Patrese
Williams
1'32"795
(147,422)

T. Boutsen
Williams
1'32"795
(147,422)

M. Gugelmin
Leyton
1'33"324
(146,586)

L. Perez Sala
Minardi
1'33"724
(145,960)

N. Piquet
Lotus
1'33"745
(145,928)

G. Tarquini
Ags
1'33"790
(145,858)

C. Danner
Rial
1'33"848
(145,768)

A. Senna
Mc Laren
1'30"108
(151,818)

A. Nannini
Benetton
1'31"799
(149,021)

M. Brundle
Brabham
1'31"960
(148,760)

S. Modena
Brabham
1'32"286
(148,235)

M. Alboreto
Tyrrell
1'32"491
(147,906)

I. Capelli
Leyton
1'32"493
(147,903)

A. De Cesaris
Bms Dallara
1'32"649
(147,654)

P.L. Martini
Minardi
1'33"031
(147,048)

E. Cheever
Arrows
1'33"214
(146,759)

S. Johansson
Onyx
1'33"370
(146,514)

J. Palmer
Tyrrell
1'33"741
(145,934)

S. Nakajima
Lotus
1'33"782
(145,870)

J. Herbert
Benetton
1'33"806
(145,833)

With the Mexican event over with, everthing was loaded on trucks and the convoy took off for Phoenix, Arizona. That one-week stopover in Phoenix was to see a Grand Prix racing event held in a typical western atmosphere, with an average temperature of 107 degrees Fah. and - thank God! - an average relative humidity of 10 percent, which made the heat almost tolerable.

A few days in Phoenix couldn't change what had taken place in Mexico. Furthermore, this Phoenix city track was something new for everbody, and all the adjustments - transmission ratio, suspensions, aerodynamics, and so on - could not be checked out and had to be played by ear.

The adjustments and aerodynamics actually had little importance in this kind of race; all the importance was concentrated on brakes and acceleration, and the cars with greater horsepower fared better on this track. But opportunities were also there for an outsider to score, because there was the increased possibility of a driver having to drop out because of the excessive heat and sheer physical fatigue.

Alain Prost, surprisingly enough, did very well in this race, probably because of his extensive experience in tuning-up his car to suit particular track characteristics. In the time trials, Senna grabbed it all and put everybody in their place.

Alessandro Nannini seemed to have taken quite well to this track and got the 3rd line-up position in front of the Ferrari, and Alex Caffi - Scuderia Italia - surprised

everybody by taking the 5th position.

There were no disappointments except that Senna had to drop out, leaving Prost to play the professor and win his "nth Grand Prix," his 36th, thus making Stewart's old record of 27 fade more distantly into the background.

There were some interesting things going on back there in Prost's dust.

For example, the two Ferraris disappearing from view, presumably because of transmission problems because no one can be really certain anymore why they do have these drop-out problems. Riccardo Patrese, at the wheel of his Williams-Renault, chalked up his second straight 2nd place, which was very significant considering that the Williams still had the same old chassis.

Then Cheevers, a hometown boy (he's from Pheonix), gave us a beautiful show, even though his Arrows still doesn't give him the kind of arm freedom he really needs for doing his best driving.

The presentation of the two Dallaras of the Scuderia Italia had people arguing. Caffi was in 3rd position and trying to lap his teammate De Cesaris for the second time, but De Cesaris didn't see him and Caffi wound up against the wall. They were both pretty angry with each other about it, and so were the team managers.

Besides Patrese's 2nd place, there was also great rejoicing in the Williams-Renault camp over Boutsen's 6th place. This Belgium driver's been having a tough time getting that same touch he had when he was with Benetton (when he would often go faster than Nannini).

We were filled with both doubts and expectations regarding this new track because our bad impressions of Detroit were still fresh in our minds. This new track is located in the Monument Valley of the Grand Canyon and isn't very long. It's really quite fascinating, with the cactus and all. We weren't at all disappointed with it. It's a beautiful track, has a beautiful atmosphere about it and it's modern without being impersonal.

I'm not so sure about how safe it is with its immovable walls and obstacles. Anyway, it's fun driving on it although it can be a little monotonous.

Being on the edge of the desert, it's a very hot place. But it's a dry heat and really not all that uncomfortable. The heat does, however, cause some technical difficulties.

It's interesting to note how the various drivers tried to cope with the heat. Some stuffed their suits and helmets with cooling substances, while others took along some chilled drinking water. All in all, it's really a nice track.

Gabriele Tarquini

The first F1 event in the States was held in 1959 at the Sebring track, famous for its long-duration races. It was held in Riverside the following year, and in 1961 the race was held at Watkins Glen, which was far from being ideal. First of all, it was a poor location geographically, and then it was completely unsuited for F1 racing, both from the technical and safety points of view.

In 1976, Formula 1 debuted in the city of Long Beach, California - which is a continuation of Los Angeles - thus making two Grand Prix in the U.S.A. This initiative was a rather successful attempt to establish a sort of American Monte Carlo, but in 1984 the promoters switched their interest to the more powerful Indy car Formula.

Meanwhile the Watkins Glen Grand Prix was replaced by the one in Detroit, Michigan, which was also a city track that ran through the heart of the world's automobile manufacturing capital.

There have been other wealthy and enthusiastic Formula 1 promoters in the U.S. In fact, in 1981 and '82, the races were held in Las Vegas on a track that was staked off in the hotel parking area of Ceasar's Palace, the famous gambling mecca and the place that hosts world-championship boxing events. A decidedly disappointing attempt was also made to establish the race at Dallas, but only one Formula 1 race was held there.

The Detroit race was also shelved, and so this year they're going to make a try at Phoenix. The small city is located in the middle of a desert. The climate's rather nice in the wintertime, but you can't be without air-conditioning in the summertime, unless you're a lizard. However, it's a well laid-out city, and the speed-circus managers found it had interesting possibilities.

The city managers have decided to invest about 4 billion lire in the project, and they've signed with the International Federation for one race each year for 5 years running.

Cheever, s hometown lad, came in a very fine 3rd, nicely defending his come, country's colours.

Prost, perfect as usual, between palm trees, buildings and tires

Facing page: after a hot day at the track, the "circus" protagonists have some fun, western style.
The new Minardi, having only just made its debut in the previous race, is still having growing pains.

FINISHING ORDER

	DRIVER	CAR	AVERAGE	DELAY
1.	**Alain Prost**	McLaren	140.680	
2.	**Riccardo Patrese**	Williams	139.919	39"696
3.	**Eddie Cheever**	Arrows	139.852	43"210
4.	**Christian Danner**	Rial Arc	138.034	1 lap
5.	**Johnny Herbert**	Benetton	137.363	1 lap
6.	**Thierry Boutsen**	Williams	136.882	1 lap
7.	**Gabriele Tarquini**	Ags	136.990	2 laps
8.	**Andrea De Cesaris**	Bms Dallara	137.795	5 laps
9.	**Jonathan Palmer**	Tyrrell	139.681	6 laps

RETIREMENTS

DRIVER	CAR	LAPS	REASON
Philippe Alliot	Lola	3	Spin
Derek Warwick	Arrows	7	Accident
Alessandro Nannini	Benetton	10	Drop-out
Michele Alboreto	Tyrrell	17	Gearbox
Mauricio Gugelmin	Leyton	20	Disqualified
Ivan Capelli	Leyton	22	Transmission
Satoru Nakajima	Lotus	24	Accelerator
Pier Luigi Martini	Minardi	26	Engine
Nigel Mansell	Ferrari	31	Electrical system
Stefano Modena	Brabham	37	Brakes
Martin Brundle	Brabham	43	Brakes
Ayrton Senna	McLaren	44	Ignition
Luis Perez Sala	Minardi	46	Engine
Stefan Johansson	Onyx	50	Suspension
Nelson Piquet	Lotus	52	Accident
Alex Caffi	Bms Dallara	52	Accident
Gerhard Berger	Ferrari	61	Electrical system

BEST LAPS

DRIVER AND CAR	LAP	TIME	AVERAGE
Senna (McLaren)	38	1'33"969	145.580
Prost (McLaren)	32	1'34"957	144.065
De Cesaris (Bms Dallara)	64	1'35"155	143.765
Mansell (Ferrari)	24	1'35"168	143.746
Caffi (Bms Dallara)	50	1'35"291	143.560
Palmer (Tyrrell)	50	1'35"349	143.473
Johansson (Onyx)	49	1'35"435	143.344
Boutsen (Williams)	61	1'35"526	143.207
Cheever (Arrows)	64	1'35"650	143.021
Piquet (Lotus)	48	1'35"837	142.742
Berger (Ferrari)	33	1'35"930	142.604
Patrese (Williams)	63	1'35"973	142.540
Alboreto (Tyrrell)	17	1'36"140	142.292
Modena (Brabham)	19	1'36"213	142.185
Brundle (Brabham)	19	1'36"391	141.922
Capelli (Leyton)	19	1'36"722	141.436
Danner (Rial Arc)	61	1'36"901	141.175
Nannini (Benetton)	3	1'37"134	140.836
Tarquini (Ags)	68	1'37"216	140.718
Herbert (Benetton)	49	1'37"287	140.615
Nakajima (Lotus)	22	1'37"415	140.430
Martini (Minardi)	16	1'38"135	139.400
Warwick (Arrows)	3	1'38"223	139.275
Alliot (Lola)	3	1'38"690	138.616
Gugelmin (Leyton)	6	1'38"762	138.515
Sala (Minardi)	39	1'39"506	137.479

G.P. CANADA

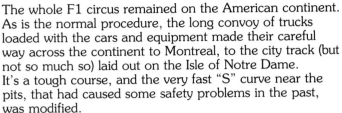

A. Senna
Mc Laren
1'21"049
(194,993)

G. Berger
Ferrari
1'21"946
(192,859)

T. Boutsen
Williams
1'22"311
(192,004)

A. Caffi
Bms Dallara
1'22"901
(190,637)

P. Alliot
Lola
1'23"059
(190,274)

D. Warwick
Arrows
1'23"348
(189,615)

J. Palmer
Tyrrell
1'23"665
(188,896)

E. Cheever
Arrows
1'23"828
(188,529)

S. Johansson
Onyx
1'23"979
(188,190)

M. Alboreto
Tyrrell
1'24"296
(187,482)

R. Arnoux
Ligier
1'24"558
(186,901)

L. Perez Sala
Minardi
1'24"786
(186,399)

R. Moreno
Coloni
1'25"037
(185,849)

A. Prost
Mc Laren
1'20"973
(195,176)

R. Patrese
Williams
1'21"165
(193,243)

N. Mansell
Ferrari
1'22"165
(192,345)

S. Modena
Brabham
1'22"612
(191,304)

A. De Cesaris
Bms Dallara
1'23"050
(190,295)

P.L. Martini
Minardi
1'23"252
(189,833)

A. Nannini
Benetton
1'23"542
(189,174)

N. Larini
Osella
1'23"799
(188,594)

M. Gugelmin
Leyton
1'23"863
(188,450)

N. Piquet
Lotus
1'24"029
(188,078)

I. Capelli
Leyton
1'24"406
(187,238)

C. Danner
Rial
1'24"727
(186,529)

G. Tarquini
Ags
1'24"793
(186,383)

The whole F1 circus remained on the American continent. As is the normal procedure, the long convoy of trucks loaded with the cars and equipment made their careful way across the continent to Montreal, to the city track (but not so much so) laid out on the Isle of Notre Dame.

It's a tough course, and the very fast "S" curve near the pits, that had caused some safety problems in the past, was modified.

Just like it happened last year, all the drivers got there without having been able to run tests, so the drivers that had better testing capabilities probably had a slight advantage.

The starting line-up was very interesting and is worth a few comments.

Prost's time run was only 1/10th faster than Senna's, but it was an important difference. Prost was complaining about the material the team had furnished him. The Brazilian's superiority was taken for granted, but Prost was not about to buy that.

Patrese - who had placed 2nd twice and had 12 world points - got the 3rd best trials time and was in the 2nd row. His car was evidently competitive, but Riccardo was well aware that Williams - and Renault, especially - were already seriously negotiating to get Alain Prost for 1990. Prost wants out of McLaren, and Renault sees this a perfect opportunity for them. The sacrificial lamb, of course, would be Riccardo Patrese.

Berger, who had completely recouperated from his

accident at Imola, made better time than Mansell had, and was next to Patrese in the 2nd row. Strangely enough, the three drivers that were changing teams were faster than those remaining on the teams: Senna, Mansell and Boutsen.
The Phoenix outsiders - Modena, Caffi, De Cesaris, and Martini - were still up in the first rows.
The Pirelli tires contributed to the performance of these outsiders. This year was Pirelli's racing comeback, and it accordingly signed contracts with several teams to get some experience and to also demonstrate its intentions and professional capabilities.
At that time, the most competitive teams were Brabham, Dallara and Minardi. But the weather changed all the forecasts. It was raining cats and dogs. Right off the bat, Mansell gets the black flag for leaving the pit in an illegal manner. Prost is scared silly by the wet track, which is the normal reaction for him. Senna wants everyone to realize that he's the king of the wet track, and therefore gets way out in front. But surprise, surprise! Two laps from the end of the race, he lost his crown to Boutsen.
Patrese was definitely faster than Boutsen, but the flat under part of his Williams started coming loose, and he had to be satisfied with 2nd place, which made it his third straight 2nd place.
All we can say about that is "poor Richard."
Andrea De Cesaris was happy on the podium with his 3rd place award, and the tear of joy flowed along with the champagne.

I really like this track with its fast sections, slow curves and dangerous fast curves that require a lot of fast braking followed by fast, full-power acceleration. It also has two chicanes which are really not true chicanes. However, this track lets you do your best driving. Last year I got a very very good impression of this track, and I well remember that I was in the best position right up to just a few laps from the finish. Then my transmission started acting up.
As I say, I like the track an awful lot because it lets a drive show what he can really do.

Stefano Modena

Frank Williams is not what you would call a lucky man. Were it not for his iron will he would never have been able to overcome all of his adversaries and his bad luck.

For years he's managed to exist on the fringes of the golden Formula 1 world, always on the lookout for a prospective sponsor or financer who could back him and give his stable a decided boost in quality.

In the '70s along came the Arabs, and they solved his financial problems and gave him his opportunity to makethe big quality jump, and he did. In fact, in 1980, Alan Jones won his first world title for him, and then Keke Rosberg did a repeat for him in 1982.

Frank was shrewd enough to realize that the Honda engine had an enormous potential. He was way ahead of everybody else on this. He signed with Honda in 1983. His team had to sweat it out for a couple of seasons, but the rewards finally came.

Poor Frank had a terrible car accident right before the start of the '86 season, and he was confined to a wheelchair.

Despite this problem he turned a deaf ear to the many who suggested he sell out. After a triumphal 1987, and Honda decided to sign with the McLaren and Lotus, he was still to continue upstream in his progress.

The less powerful Judd engine he had to revert to during the next season gave meager results, but Frank laid the groundwork for a

sensational comeback. He got Renault to give him an exclusive for his return to the Formula 1. It was a rainy Sunday on the Gilles Villeneuve track in Montreal that the English-French combination produced it first sweet fruit, and this combination promised even further successes. In fact, one followed shortly after with Boutsen and Patrese scoring a double-header, Boutsen 1st and Patrese 2nd, an unexpected triumph.

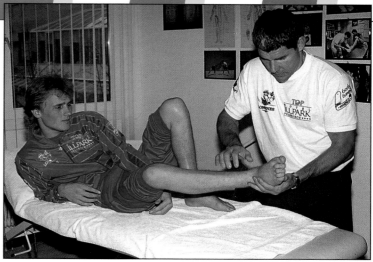

Johnny Herbert didn't qualify for the Canadian Grand Prix, and now Tony Matis is helping him completely recover from his Formula 3000 accident.

Susy and Simone - Riccardo Patrese's wife and son - watch Riccardo come in second after he'd led the pack for three-quarters of the race.

The newlyweds: Nicola and Barbara Larini! Nicola wanted to give his new bride a nice wedding present, but his on-board computer let him down when he was in third postion.

FINISHING ORDER

	DRIVER	CAR	AVERAGE	DELAY
1.	**Thierry Boutsen**	Williams	149.707	
2.	**Riccardo Patrese**	Williams	149.093	30"007
3.	**Andrea De Cesaris**	Bms Dallara	147.747	1'36"649
4.	**Nelson Piquet**	Lotus	147.650	1'41"484
5.	**René Arnoux**	Ligier	145.613	1 lap
6.	**Alex Caffi**	Bms Dallara	144.928	2 laps
7.	**Ayrton Senna**	McLaren	150.050	3 laps
8.	**Christian Danner**	Rial Arc	142.349	3 laps

RETIREMENTS

DRIVER	CAR	LAPS	REASON
Alessandro Nannini	Benetton	0	Ruled out
Nigel Mansell	Ferrari	0	Ruled out
Michele Alboreto	Tyrrell	0	Electrical system
Stefano Modena	Brabham	0	Accident
Pier Luigi Martini	Minardi	0	Accident
Alain Prost	McLaren	2	Suspension system
Eddie Cheever	Arrows	3	Accident
Gabriele Tarquini	Ags	6	Accident
Gerhard Berger	Ferrari	6	Gearbox
Mauricio Gugelmin	Leyton	11	Electrical system
Luis Perez Sala	Minardi	11	Off track
Stefan Johansson	Onyx	13	Ruled out
Philippe Alliot	Lola	26	Off track
Ivan Capelli	Leyton	28	Off track
Nicola Larini	Osella	33	Electrical system
Jonathan Palmer	Tyrrell	35	Off track
Derek Warwick	Arrows	40	Engine
Roberto Moreno	Coloni	57	Differential

BEST LAPS

DRIVER AND CAR	LAP	TIME	AVERAGE
Palmer (Tyrrell)	11	1'31"925	171.923
Senna (McLaren)	15	1'32"143	171.516
Piquet (Lotus)	11	1'32"422	170.998
De Cesaris (Bms Dallara)	11	1'32"481	170.889
Capelli (Leyton)	14	1'32"742	170.408
Caffi (Bms Dallara)	15	1'33"167	169.631
Boutsen (Williams)	14	1'33"790	168.504
Gugelmin (Leyton)	11	1'34"231	167.716
Sala (Minardi)	10	1'34"509	167.222
Patrese (Williams)	15	1'35"251	165.920
Johansson (Onyx)	10	1'35"333	165.777
Moreno (Coloni)	13	1'35"369	165.714
Larini (Osella)	11	1'35"726	165.096
Danner (Rial Arc)	11	1'35"970	164.676
Warwick (Arrows)	15	1'36"443	163.869
Alliot (Lola)	11	1'36"687	163.455
Arnoux (Ligier)	11	1'37"131	162.708
Berger (Ferrari)	6	1'37"916	161.404
Tarquini (Ags)	5	1'38"284	160.799
Cheever (Arrows)	3	1'38"631	160.234
Prost (McLaren)	1	1'41"751	155.320

G.P. FRANCIA

A. Senna
Mc Laren
1'07"228
(204,183)

A. Nannini
Benetton
1'08"137
(201,459)

G. Berger
Ferrari
1'08"233
(201,175)

R. Patrese
Williams
1'08"993
(198,959)

M. Gugelmin
Leyton
1'09"036
(198,835)

I. Capelli
Leyton
1'09"283
(198,127)

M. Donnelly
Arrows
1'09"524
(197,440)

J. Alesi
Tyrrell
1'09"668
(197,032)

R. Arnoux
Ligier
1'10"077
(195,882)

N. Piquet
Lotus
1'10"135
(195,720)

S. Modena
Brabham
1'10"254
(195,338)

E. Pirro
Benetton
1'10"292
(195,283)

A. Caffi
Bms Dallara
1'10"468
(194,795)

A. Prost
Mc Laren
1'07"203
(204,259)

N. Mansell
Ferrari
1'07"455
(203,496)

T. Boutsen
Williams
1'08"211
(201,240)

P. Alliot
Lola
1'08"561
(200,213)

J. Palmer
Tyrrell
(1'09"026
(198,864)

B. Gachot
Onyx
1'09"122
(198,588)

S. Johansson
Onyx
1'09"299
(198,081)

E. Bernard
Lola
1'09"596
(197,235)

O. Grouillard
Ligier
1'09"596
(196,893)

S. Nakajima
Lotus
1'10"119
(195,764)

G. Tarquini
Ags
1'10"216
(195,494)

P.L. Martini
Minardi
1'10"267
(195,352)

E. Cheever
Arrows
1'10"372
(195,061)

Prost confirmed that he's quitting McLaren, but he hadn't yet decided who he'd race for. Everybody knew he was sure to join the "Williams-Renault" team; who else? It was already taken for granted that Berger would step in as soon as he left, but this was still to be announced. Meanwhile, Patrese seemed the likely Ferrari candidate. He's got grit, determination, a will to win, and lots and lots of experience.

Prost was again faster than Senna, with only 25 thousandths of a second difference, followed by a particularly aggressive Mansell. The race promised to be a heated battle. The score at this seventh event was significant: 27 points for Senna with 3 victories, and 29 for Prost with 5 placings but only one victory. Patrese was 3rd with 18 points, but it looked like the fight for the title would again only be a McLaren problem.

The year of study for the Italian manufacturer should be precisely dedicated to eliminating the problem of tire performance inconsistency both in the time trials and races, so that they'll no longer represent a handicap for the top teams. France was also the setting for the Tyrrell-Alboreto-problem nativity scene. Figuring "business is business," Ken Tyrrell grabbed onto a sponsor without having first consulted Michele Alboreto, and the sponsor promptly bumped Michele and he became a little bitter because he was just starting to get some good performance out of the car. Tyrrell got a replacement ready well in advance and had him right out on the track ready to step in if necessary. His name was Jean Alesi, a fast driver from France who had raced in the F. 3000 championship events. Tyrrell hired him outright (signed him up for three years) and practically left Michele out in the cold.

There were two starts to this race. In the first one, Gugelmin took off like an acrobat; and when he had to put on the brakes, he came to a grinding stop, upside-down. Then there was the second start, which went better, except that Senna didn't even make it to the first curve because he lost his transmission, differential and brakes. Prost got all ready for his 37th victory, while Mansell's 2nd place made everybody at Ferrari (including Cesare Fiorio) heave a sigh of relief, and Patrese came in 3rd all alone. It was his first 3rd placing after three straight 2nd placings. Alesi came in 4th and all the French flags were waving like crazy.

When I got that call before the Grand Prix and was offered the job with Tyrrell, I was a little scared to accept at first but then I said O.K. During the tests, when the Tyrrell pit crew informed me my time was about 1 minute and 14 seconds, I thought: "Jesus, I'm standing still!" So I changed my attitude, got more confident and began following the more famous drivers like Patrese. About that time I realized I was actually going faster than he was and that I could pass him, which I did. Boy, was that satisfying! The race itself started off with a few accidents and we had to have a restart which went O.K. After about 10 laps I was behind Palmer my teammate, and shortly thereafter I passed him. Then I saw the pits signal me: "2nd Position." Wow! I couldn't believe it. I was in 2nd place.! Frankly it took about 3 or 4 turns to get my excitement back under control. I slipped back a bit as the race went on, but did manage to come in 4th. My crew in the pits were wild about my performance.

Jean Alesi

On the occasion of the French Grand Prix, which is the one Alain Prost considers "his" Grand Prix, Alain called a press conference to officially announce the fact that he and McLaren were through. He earned his first point right at his debut in Argentina, which augured an outstanding career.

But that McLaren car was not the car it is today and at the end of his first season, Prost was in 15th place with only 5 points.

During the next three years Alain raced for the Renault team and racked up several victories and pole positions. In 1983 he came close to winning the world title. Then the polemics started and down came the final curtain: the divorce.

But there was McLaren again holding out its hand to Prost. They didn't offer him much but he could race for a team that was completely different from the one with which he had debuted back in 1980.

Prost was lucky to have joined McLaren in 1984 and he became as big a protagonist as his teammate Niki Lauda. When Lauda became the world champion, Prost was only behind him by half a point.

Then, the following season, after an interesting duel with Michele Alboredo, Prost finally won the world title and he did it in the style of a true champion.

He did it again in 1986, but it was a tough battle. He had to deal with two very determined Williams drivers, Mansell and Piquet, who also had the advantage of the high-powered Honda engines, but in the very last race Prost poured it on and came out the winner.

After a rather muted year, the McLaren came back as full of vigor as ever, but Prost's new teammate, the formidable Ayrton Senna, proved more than a match for him.

In the early part of the season that just came to a close, Alain Prost and Ayrton Senna become "alienated" and it steadily got worse until it reached the breaking point. The inevitable divorce ensued with Prost making the announcement in France and subsequently signing with Ferrari for 1990.

A fine showing by four rookies. They all qualified, ran a good race, and Alesi even won points.
Prost announces it officially: he's leaving McLaren.
A great comeback by Mansell after having been last to leave the pits.

FINISHING ORDER

	DRIVER	CAR	AVERAGE	DELAY
1.	**Alain Prost**	McLaren	185.830	
2.	**Nigel Mansell**	Ferrari	184.456	44"017
3.	**Riccardo Patrese**	Williams	183.749	1'06"921
4.	**Jean Alesi**	Tyrrell	183.555	1'13"232
5.	**Stefan Johansson**	Onyx	183.035	1 lap
6.	**Olivier Grouillard**	Ligier	202.921	1 lap
7.	**Eddie Cheever**	Arrows	181.294	1 lap
8.	**Nelson Piquet**	Lotus	180.953	2 laps
9.	**Emanuele Pirro**	Benetton	180.924	2 laps
10.	**Jonathan Palmer**	Tyrrell	179.616	2 laps
11.	**Eric Bernard**	Lola	181.876	3 laps
12.	**Martin Donnelly**	Arrows	177.456	3 laps
13.	**Bertrand Gachot**	Onyx	174.685	4 laps

BEST LAPS

DRIVER AND CAR	LAP	TIME	AVERAGE
Gugelmin (Leyton)	29	1'12"090	190.412
Nannini (Benetton)	26	1'12"406	189.581
Prost (McLaren)	38	1'12"500	189.335
Mansell (Ferrari)	75	1'12"542	189.226
Piquet (Lotus)	66	1'12"723	188.755
Capelli (Leyton)	30	1'12"737	188.718
Boutsen (Williams)	3	1'12"755	188.672
Berger (Ferrari)	4	1'12"937	188.201
Alesi (Tyrrell)	52	1'12"964	188.131
Patrese (Williams)	37	1'12"977	188.098
Bernard (Lola)	55	1'13"144	187.668
Cheever (Arrows)	41	1'13"171	187.599
Johansson (Onyx)	55	1'13"175	187.589
Palmer (Tyrrell)	49	1'13"262	187.366
Gachot (Onyx)	34	1'13"358	187.121
Grouillard (Ligier)	36	1'13"399	187.016
Nakajima (Lotus)	42	1'13"657	186.361
Pirro (Benetton)	75	1'13"712	186.222
Alliot (Lola)	3	1'13"719	186.204
Modena (Brabham)	64	1'14"137	185.155
Donnelly (Arrows)	39	1'14"538	184.158
Martini (Minardi)	29	1'14"631	183.929
Caffi (Bms Dallara)	21	1'14"789	183.540
Arnoux (Ligier)	4	1'14"956	183.131
Tarquini (Ags)	4	1'15"437	181.964

RETIREMENTS

DRIVER	CAR	LAPS	REASON
Ayrton Senna	McLaren	0	Differential
René Arnoux	Ligier	14	Gearbox
Alex Caffi	Bms Dallara	27	Clutch
Gerhard Berger	Ferrari	29	Gearbox
Gabriele Tarquini	Ags	30	Engine
Philippe Alliot	Lola	30	Engine
Pier Luigi Martini	Minardi	31	Engine
Alessandro Nannini	Benetton	40	Rear left suspension
Ivan Capelli	Leyton	47	Engine
Satoru Nakajima	Lotus	49	Electrical system
Thierry Boutsen	Williams	50	Gearbox
Stefano Modena	Brabham	67	Engine
Mauricio Gugelmin	Leyton	71	Not classified

G.P. GRAN BRETAGNA

A. Prost
Mc Laren
1'09"266
(248,330)

G. Berger
Ferrari
1'09"855
(246,236)

M. Gugelmin
Leyton
1'10"336
(246,236)

I. Capelli
Leyton
1'10"650
(243,465)

N. Plquet
Lotus
1'10"925
(242,521)

P. Alliot
Lola
1'11"541
(240,433)

S. Modena
Brabham
1'11"755
(239,716)

S. Nakajima
Lotus
1'11"960
(239,033)

J. Palmer
Tyrrell
1'12"070
(238,668)

M. Brundle
Brabham
1'12"327
(237,820)

J. Alesi
Tyrrell
1'12"341
(237,774)

O. Grouillard
Ligier
1'12"605
(236,909)

E. Pirro
Benetton
1'13"148
(235,151)

A. Senna
Mc Laren
1'09"099
(248,930)

N. Mansell
Ferrari
1'09"488
(247,536)

R. Patrese
Williams
1'09"865
(246,201)

T. Boutsen
Williams
1'10"376
(244,413)

A. Nannini
Benetton
1'10"798
(242,956)

P.L. Martini
Minardi
1'11"368
(241,016)

E. Bernard
Lola
1'11"687
(239,943)

L. Perez Sala
Minardi
1'11"826
(239,479)

N. Larini
Osella
1'12"061
(238,698)

D. Warwick
Arrows
1'12"208
(238,212)

B. Gachot
Onyx
1'12"329
(237,813)

R. Moreno
Coloni
(1'12"412
(237,541)

A. De Cesaris
Bms Dallara
1'12"904
(235,938)

This championship was all-McLaren once again, but it didn't dominate it as much as it had in 1988.

The crazy thing that happened was that Alain Prost declared he wasn't happy with the way the McLaren was treating him and had decided to leave. His complaint was that Senna was getting preferential treatment. Moreover, he implied that the team didn't want him to win the championship, and that he had gone out and won races, and topped the list with eleven more points than his Brazilian teammate had, and that Senna was almost in the position of having to watch out for Patrese's threat with his 22 world-classification points.

If this were true, just imagine how mad the people who don't want him to win the title must be!

In any case, the English Grand Prix featured the definitive presentation of the McLaren MP 4/5 in its total configuration: with the transversely-mounted transmission, for which it was originally designed.

The new 89 chassis was gradually developed on the track in definite phases until it reached its final form at Silverstone, a very fast track with large difficult curves, where weight, overhang, aerdynamics and tuning are more important than they are on other tracks.

The transverse transmission, however, complicated things a bit with regard to the oil system. In fact, during the two days of testing the McLaren seemed to have had it. What was happening was that inertial forces on the curves would affect lubrication efficiency so badly the car was in trouble after just two or three laps.

They were all ready to switch back to the traditional transmission and rear suspension system. But Ron Dennis stuck to his guns. His calmness and confidence put the entire team in the right frame of mind and no one panicked. At the Sunday-morning warm-up at 10 a.m., the car was ready to go, and after just a few laps, it became clear that the problem had been solved.

But the Ferrari was close by, and the McLaren knew it would have keep its guard up.

At the start, it was Senna and Prost as usual, with Berger and Mansell staying in their wake for a short distance. Senna was ripping along like a rocket, with Prost right on his tail. Then came the big surprise: Senna muffs a braking maneuver on the Stowe Corner turn, loses control, and goes off into the sand. And that was all for him. He may have had some technical difficulty with the rear end. So Prost lucked out again. The rest of the race was a breeze for him. He came in 1st with no trouble at all, leaving 2nd honors to Mansell (which definitely convinced Fiorio and Co. at Ferrari that they were doing things right).

Racing at Silvestone means racing on one of the world's most difficult permanent tracks. Those with a lot of experience have taught me that the track looks easy but is actually very difficult, both from the standpoint of the driver's physical stamina and of the car's set-up condition. I have always remembered these words and this has helped me from making mistakes.
This year I got my best F1 result: 5th place. Of course, we were all very proud of this; myself, the team, our friends, and all those others who had always helped and taught me to properly "interpret" this track which still is, in my mind, one of the most spectacular tracks in the world.

Pier Luigi Martini

It was on this classic Silverstone track, in one of the most prestigious Grand Prix events, that Minardi had its "golden hour". This well-liked team from Romagna did a very unexpected and almost miraculous thing: it won three points, thanks to Martini's 5th place and Sala's 6th. With these two placings, Minardi was able to keep from slipping back into the group of teams that were obliged to undergo and pass the pre-qualification tests.

It was also further proof that Italian racing is no longer the exclusive specialty of the Ferrari. In fact, in addition to the Ferrari team - and, of course, the Minardi team - the others that participated in the F1 world championships (and took turns at having their share of luck) included Osella, Italia, Coloni, Eurobrun (half Swiss), and Benetton (English from the technical point of view).

Minardi made its first F1 appearance in 1985 and it was tough going to get anyone to pay attention to them, much less build up a following of fans. For three long seasons they didn't earn one single point. Then at Detroit, in 1988, Pierluigi Martini came in 6th. This result was particularly significant because after having taken his first toddling steps in the Grand Prix world with Minardi, he had made his return to F1 racing with this same team.

Although Giancarlo Minardi started out with very low capital his love was so great for the sport that he couldn't help but succeed in setting up quite a respectable team for himself. Not everyone would have had his stick-to-itiveness. And he never faltered once in pursuing his goal. Now in 1989 his intelligent policy is beginning to pay off with good placings and interesting performance results in practice.

The Minardi team has always earned admiration for the way it has patiently carved out a place for itself in Formula 1 by sheer willpower and knowing how to get along with others.

There were plenty of people who doubted the team's technical growth potential but maybe they didn't stop to realize that this was a team whose roots were in Romagna, that place where "engines" are worshipped like pagan gods.

At the first curve, the McLaren is already out in front.

Silverstone: where Speed is King.

FINISHING ORDER

	DRIVER	CAR	AVERAGE	DELAY
1.	**Alain Prost**	McLaren	231.168	
2.	**Nigel Mansell**	Ferrari	230.231	19"369
3.	**Alessandro Nannini**	Benetton	228.860	48"019
4.	**Nelson Piquet**	Lotus	227.973	1'06"735
5.	**Pier Luigi Martini**	Minardi	225.945	1 lap
6.	**Luis Perez Sala**	Minardi	225.646	1 lap
7.	**Olivier Grouillard**	Ligier	225.606	1 lap
8.	**Satoru Nakajima**	Lotus	224.378	1 lap
9.	**Derek Warwick**	Arrows	223.841	2 laps
10.	**Thierry Boutsen**	Williams	223.641	2 laps
11.	**Emanuele Pirro**	Benetton	222.892	2 laps
12.	**Bertrand Gachot**	Onyx	222.113	2 laps

RETIREMENTS

DRIVER	CAR	LAPS	REASON
Roberto Moreno	Coloni	2	Engine
Ayrton Senna	McLaren	11	Accident
Andrea De Cesaris	Bms Dallara	14	Engine
Ivan Capelli	Leyton	15	Transmission
Riccardo Patrese	Williams	19	Accident
Nicola Larini	Osella	23	Drop-out
Jean Alesi	Tyrrell	28	Accident
Stefano Modena	Brabham	31	Engine
Jonathan Palmer	Tyrrell	32	Accident
Philippe Alliot	Lola	39	Engine
Eric Bernard	Lola	46	Engine
Gerhard Berger	Ferrari	49	Gearbox
Martin Brundle	Brabham	49	Engine
Mauricio Gugelmin	Leyton	54	Transmission

BEST LAPS

DRIVER AND CAR	LAP	TIME	AVERAGE
Mansell (Ferrari)	57	1'12"017	238.844
Prost (McLaren)	58	1'12"193	238.261
Nannini (Benetton)	54	1'12"397	237.590
Berger (Ferrari)	29	1'13"477	234.098
Piquet (Lotus)	55	1'13"565	233.818
Gugelmin (Leyton)	27	1'13"735	233.279
Senna (McLaren)	10	1'13"737	233.272
Capelli (Leyton)	8	1'14"224	231.742
Boutsen (Williams)	57	1'14"248	231.667
Martini (Minardi)	55	1'14"388	231.231
Grouillard (Ligier)	54	1'14"446	231.051
Gachot (Onyx)	62	1'14"484	230.933
Sala (Minardi)	61	1'14"492	230.908
Nakajima (Lotus)	57	1'14"720	230.203
Pirro (Benetton)	61	1'15"293	228.452
Brundle (Brabham)	49	1'15"343	228.300
Warwick (Arrows)	60	1'15"443	227.997
Modena (Brabham)	31	1'15"489	227.858
Alliot (Lola)	34	1'15"495	227.840
Alesi (Tyrrell)	26	1'15"519	227.768
Palmer (Tyrrell)	27	1'15"931	226.532
Bernard (Lola)	4	1'16"264	225.543
Patrese (Williams)	17	1'16"586	224.595
Larini (Osella)	22	1'16"981	223.442
De Cesaris (Bms Dallara)	3	1'18"076	220.308
Moreno (Coloni)	2	1'20"498	213.680

A. Prost
Mc Laren
1'43"295
(236,887)

G. Berger
Ferrari
1'44"467
(234,229)

T. Boutsen
Williams
1'44"702
(233,703)

N. Piquet
Lotus
1'45"475
(231,991)

J. Alesi
Tyrrell
1'46"888
(228,924)

M. Brundle
Brabham
1'47"216
(228,223)

M. Gugelmin
Leyton
1'47"387
(227,860)

S. Modena
Brabham
1'47"511
(227,597)

S. Nakajima
Lotus
1'47"663
(227,276)

A. Caffi
Bms Dallara
1'47"679
(227,242)

I. Capelli
Leyton
1'48"078
(226,403)

S. Johansson
Onyx
1'48"348
(225,839)

M. Alboreto
Lola
1'48"670
(225,170)

A. Senna
Mc Laren
1'42"300
(239,191)

N. Mansell
Ferrari
1'44"020
(235,236)

R. Patrese
Williams
1'44"511
(234,130)

A. Nannini
Benetton
1'45"033
(232,967)

E. Pirro
Benetton
1'45"845
(231,180)

O. Grouillard
Ligier
1'46"893
(228,913)

P.L. Martini
Minardi
1'47"380
(227,875)

P. Alliot
Lola
1'47"486
(227,650)

D. Warwick
Arrows
1'47"533
(227,551)

J. Palmer
Tyrrell
1'47"676
(227,248)

A. De Cesaris
Bms Dallara
1'47"879
(226,821)

R. Arnoux
Ligier
1'48"266
(226,010)

E. Cheever
Arrows
1'48"396
(225,739)

Being ahead by 20 points, Alain Prost could sleep peacefully. But it isn't like him not to worry. In all of his statements he says that the team can manage the results, and that makes him feel he's in difficulty.

Hockenheim is another very fast track, exceeding 230 km/h on the average. But it's different from Silverstone. The drivers say it's like a dragster strip. Braking, a 2nd and 3rd gear chicane, acceleration, braking, another chicane, etc. etc. One bend in the amphitheater is hardly enough to appeal to a driver's imagination.

Maybe because of this, or maybe because McLaren had definitely solved the engine-oil circulation problem with the transverse transmission, but the two McLaren-Hondas gave all the others a real lesson. While Prost was exactly 1 second behind Senna, Mansell was trailing by 1.7 seconds, Berger by 2.1 seconds, Patrese by 2.7 seconds, etc.! Senna won the pole position with an average speed of almost 240 km/h.

At the green light, Senna took the lead and no one could catch up to him.

Michele Alboreto was back on the track with the Lola-Lamborghini. When Michele and Forghieri were at Ferrari, they had a misunderstanding and Michele left, but they finally got back together, which led to the Lola-Lamborghini-Alboreto agreement.

The track is laid out in a nice straighforward manner, which prompted Senna to not try anything fancy and just concentrate on keeping his lead and winning.

Prost was too far ahead on points. Luckily the championship rules consider the results of only eleven out of the sixteen Grand Prix events as being valid.

Prost had too big a lead. He already had seven positive results after only eight races. Senna was only worrying about being able to finish a race.

As was expected from the results of the time trials, the McLarens came in 1st and 2nd...once again.

Mansell was still consistent and took 3rd place, while Berger was also consistent - in a negative way - and dropped out. The Austrian driver was almost at his wits end over not having yet earned a single world point. On the other hand, Ferrari felt they had their new Barnard vehicle, and that its full potential was yet to be revealed. The Ferrari-Barnard atmosphere became more relaxed, and there was new talk about his becoming permanent at Maranello when his contract expires on the 31st of October.

The only two big question marks are: who is going to be the new Ferrari driver? And where will Alain Prost go, now that Patrese is still on stand-by and Renault still hasn't made any official announcements?

I don't really like this track very much. It's got two chicanes that are pretty tight and not so nice. Then the straightaways are too long and too narrow. My recollections of this track are both good and bad. One of the good ones was when I raced on it for the first time in the new Benetton. One of the bad ones was the time I had reached a good position and was trailing Mansell when all of a sudden I found myself in a completely unexpected situation, had an accident, was retired from the race and almost got myself hurt pretty bad in the bargain. In any case most of the memories of my rather short F1 experience are linked to this track.

Emanuele Pirro

the "Misunderstanding Waltz", which was even quite embarrassing because Alboreto and Pa-trese were actually good friends. The Gordian Knot was negatively undone in September when all of the important moves in the driver market had already been made. They really made a sucker out of Alboreto. Being a realist, the Milanese driver accepted Ken Tyrrell's proposal. After all he made his F1 debut with the "lumberjack's" team; and then there was Harvey Postlethwaite, the English engineer who had worked with Michele for years at Ferrari and was now Tyrrell's engineering chief. In other words, that environment was very promising even though the team seemed to be very low on cash. Ken Tyrrell finally managed to find a sponsor. But this sponsor also insisted on having his say as regarded the drivers, which put Alboreto out of a job. Michele really got a raw deal there. A couple of Grand Prix events at home and then the comeback at Hockenheim, with all kinds of will to do it better. It's difficult to imagine what would have happened if Alboreto hadn't had such an iron-willed character. That's the only reason he was able to survive after having been Ferrari's pampered top driver for all those seasons. Michele Alboreto's comeback at the wheel of the Lola Lamborghini is the demonstration of how someone can still be in there racing for the pure love of it.

After Tyrrell had let Michele Alboreto go (for reasons that are not altogether justifiable), Larrousse gave him the opportunity of finishing the season by driving the Lola Lamborghini. And so we once again see this Milanese driver on the track in Germany. It was Friday the 28th and Alboreto had to get up pretty early, just as a lot of the other drivers had to do. Practice was scheduled to start two hours earlier than it normally does. So, there they were, 13 cars out on the track, ready for the prequalification "roulette", out of which only four made it to the Grand Prix grid. Notwithstanding all the personal satisfaction and big earnings during his nine years in F1, Michele Alboreto loves racing so much and wanted to continue so badly that he was ready to face this new obstacle and do his utmost best. Abbandoned by Ferrari in the early part of July, 1988, Michele Alboreto considered the Williams offer a golden opportunity. Frank Williams had already told him on numerous occasions that he guaranteed he would take Riccardo Patrese's place. And this started off

Senna and Steve Nickols, a winning two-some.

The Ferraris were forced to play the "hounds", with Mansell finally managing to place 3rd. Berger was unlucky again and had to drop out.

FINISHING ORDER

	DRIVER	CAR	AVERAGE	DELAY
1.	**Ayrton Senna**	McLaren	224.566	
2.	**Alain Prost**	McLaren	223.738	18"151
3.	**Nigel Mansell**	Ferrari	220.817	1'23"254
4.	**Riccardo Patrese**	Williams	218.424	1 lap
5.	**Nelson Piquet**	Lotus	217.734	1 lap
6.	**Derek Warwick**	Arrows	216.790	1 lap
7.	**Andrea De Cesaris**	Bms Dallara	216.197	1 lap
8.	**Martin Brundle**	Brabham	215.751	1 lap
9.	**Pier Luigi Martini**	Minardi	215.533	1 lap
10.	**Jean Alesi**	Tyrrell	211.391	2 laps
11.	**René Arnoux**	Ligier	205.689	3 laps
12.	**Eddie Cheever**	Arrows	215.314	5 laps

BEST LAPS

DRIVER AND CAR	LAP	TIME	AVERAGE
Senna (McLaren)	43	1'45"884	231.094
Prost (McLaren)	42	1'45"977	230.892
Mansell (Ferrari)	21	1'48"722	225.062
Berger (Ferrari)	10	1'48"931	224.630
Pirro (Benetton)	25	1'49"005	224.478
Nakajima (Lotus)	33	1'49"311	223.849
Nannini (Benetton)	4	1'49"665	223.127
Patrese (Williams)	20	1'49"910	222.629
Piquet (Lotus)	36	1'49"917	222.615
Cheever (Arrows)	34	1'50"216	222.011
Gugelmin (Leyton)	19	1'50"493	221.455
Martini (Minardi)	33	1'50"676	221.089
Alesi (Tyrrell)	30	1'50"817	220.807
Warwick (Arrows)	34	1'50"899	220.644
Brundle (Brabham)	43	1'51"012	220.419
Boutsen (Williams)	4	1'51"168	220.110
Capelli (Leyton)	30	1'51"362	219.727
De Cesaris (Bms Dallara)	31	1'51"495	219.465
Modena (Brabham)	15	1'52"562	217.384
Alliot (Lola)	19	1'52"638	217.238
Palmer (Tyrrell)	9	1'52"888	216.756
Caffi (Bms Dallara)	2	1'53"417	215.745
Johansson (Onyx)	7	1'53"686	215.235
Arnoux (Ligier)	7	1'53"907	214.817
Alboreto (Lola)	1	2'10"370	187.690

RETIREMENTS

DRIVER	CAR	LAPS	REASON
Olivier Grouillard	Ligier	0	Electrical system
Michele Alboreto	Lola	1	Electrical system
Alex Caffi	Bms Dallara	2	Engine
Thierry Boutsen	Williams	4	Accident
Alessandro Nannini	Benetton	6	Computer
Stefan Johansson	Onyx	8	Engine
Gerhard Berger	Ferrari	13	Flat tire
Jonathan Palmer	Tyrrell	16	Engine
Philippe Alliot	Lola	20	Engine
Emanuele Pirro	Benetton	26	Accident
Mauricio Gugelmin	Leyton	28	Engine
Ivan Capelli	Leyton	32	Electrical system
Satoru Nakajima	Lotus	36	Electrical system
Stefano Modena	Brabham	37	Engine

G.P. UNGHERIA

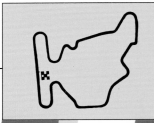

A. Senna
Mc Laren
1'20"039
(178,428)

R. Patrese
Williams
1'19"726
(179,129)

T. Boutsen
Williams
1'21"001
(176,309)

A. Caffi
Bms Dallara
1'20"704
(176,958)

G. Berger
Ferrari
1'21"270
(175,725)

A. Prost
Mc Laren
1'21"704
(176,146)

S. Modena
Brabham
1'21"472
(175,290)

A. Nannini
Benetton
1'21"076
(175,658)

P.L. Martini
Minardi
1'21"746
(174,702)

D. Warwick
Arrows
1'21"617
(174,978)

N. Mansell
Ferrari
1'21"951
(174,702)

J. Alesi
Tyrrell
1'21"799
(174,589)

I. Capelli
Leyton
1'22"088
(173,974)

M. Gugelmin
Leyton
1'22"083
(173,985)

E. Cheever
Arrows
1'22"374
(173,370)

M. Brundle
Brabham
1'22"296
(173,303)

A. De Cesaris
Bms Dallara
1'22"410
(173,295)

N. Piquet
Lotus
1'22"406
(173,303)

S. Nakajima
Lotus
1'22"630
(172,833)

J. Palmer
Tyrrell
1'22"578
(172,942)

P. Ghinzani
Osella
1'22"763
(172,555)

B. Gachot
Onyx
1'22"634
(172,825)

S. Johansson
Onyx
1'23"148
(171,756)

L. Perez Sala
Minardi
1'23"017
(172,027)

M. Alboreto
Lola
1'23"733
(170,556)

E. Pirro
Benetton
1'23"399
(171,239)

The score: 53 to 36. Prost had scored eight times out of nine races, racking up three victories and four 2nd places. Senna has won 4 races....period. He either won his races or had to drop out. The outcome of this championship seemed to be quite predictable, so why was Prost complaining? But the series continued onward and we had this race in Hungary, the only Grand Prix race ever held in one of the Eastern-Block countries, at least up to now. This track, with its new underlying philosophy, was opened up a few years and doesn't need any chicanes to keep the drivers from going too fast. The fastest time on this track averaged out at about 180 km/h.

Its particular asphalt characteristics and slow, long-radii curves pose a lot of problems. This is the kind of track that makes the McLaren act a bit odd, like there's something wrong with it, but the Senna had the right magic in his hands and chalked up some decent times, while Prost seemed to be quite lost. Riccardo Patrese made the biggest impression at the time trials at the wheel of his trusty FW 12C (1988), but this old car mounted a humdinger of a new Renault engine! Boutsen's time was all of 1.3 seconds slower than Patrese's, which gave the impression that there was something personal involved there between them. Calli, of the Dallara camp, and the Pirelli tires did very well and got the 3rd position (in the second row) ahead of Prost, Berger and Co...not bad at all! This was actually a race that no one should have missed. Right off the bat, Patrese showed one and all that

what he did at the time trials was no fluke. He took the lead and kept it for more that 50 laps, with the other top drivers just tenths and hundredths of a second behind him, snapping away at his heels. The Italian driver was under more pressure than he would have liked. But he never made an error, not even once. And he kept right in there, never hesitating for a moment.
Senna, who was always less than a second behind him, was in fact in Patrese's wake, while Prost, Berger, Caffi and Mansell - behind Senna - were doing all they could to keep the gap from widening.
Then came the big let-down, Patrese's charger konked out on the 54th lap. You could almost hear Senna let out his happy war whoop, but that yell got stuck in his throat because he got rattled when Mansell swished past him in a complicated maneuver that involved the lapping of another driver.
Mansell barreled across the finish line to win while Senna rather begrudgingly had to settle for 2nd place, although he certainly didn't refuse the six world points. Boutsen, unlike Patrese, drove along steadily, never showing any particular grit, came in before Prost and ended up on the podium.
However, Berger's score of zero world points, as well as his never having had the pleasure of seeing the checkered flag, still left a certain amount of doubt as to whether any improvement at all had actually been made.

> *I like that track because it's neither too fast nor too slow.*
> *This was my first qualification of the year.*
> *And this was the first time I could really enjoy the genuine F1 atmosphere.*
> *It's really a beautiful track, and not only that, it's close to what I believe to be the most beautiful city in Europe, and in the world for that matter: Budapest.*
> *This is why I just love going to the G.P. of Hungary.*
>
> Piercarlo Ghinzani

Riccardo Patrese made headlines and reaped lots of glory in Hungary with his fantastic pole position followed by an equally fantastic race where he was dominant until his engine blew.

This racing driver made his F1 debut in 1977 when Shadow chose him to replace the less competitive Renzo Zorzi. Patrese was recommended for this job with the Anglo-American team by the later-notorious and then shareholder of this team: Franco Ambrosio.

Riccardo is a natural-born racing driver and real sportsman. This is why he was such an excellent swimmer and skier as a teenager. He wasted a lot of time waiting for a call from Ferrari.

If he hadn't almost been promised that job he wouldn't have refused so many good offers waiting for it.

Lady Luck has also not been too kind to him. In his record book, what we find are two lonely victories that hark back to the early 1980s. He would have had many more victories if he had not been plagued with many banal inconveniences such as the kind that happened at Budpest this year when he had already practically won the race.

When he joined the Williams team last season he seemed to regain his youthful exuberance. He had plenty of motivation and lots of spunk to go with it, exactly like when he was just starting out in F1. He acts like he's out to recoup what bad luck had denied him. He's well aware of the fact that he hasn't really obtained what he truly deserves and he also knows that he's got what it takes to get his just rewards.

This weekend in Hungary saw him as the absolute protagonist and his reaction when he saw his victory slip away from him was that of a true champion. He simply shrugged his shoulders and said, "Better luck next time".

Alesi and Brundle "kiss" on the second curve.

The happy enthusiastic Ferrari fans swarmed down onto the track, just as they used to do in Austria when the Grand Prix race was held there.

FINISHING ORDER

	DRIVER	CAR	AVERAGE	DELAY
1.	**Nigel Mansell**	Ferrari	167.155	
2.	**Ayrton Senna**	McLaren	166.498	25"967
3.	**Thierry Boutsen**	Williams	166.186	38"354
4.	**Alain Prost**	McLaren	166.040	44"177
5.	**Eddie Cheever**	Arrows	166.016	45"106
6.	**Nelson Piquet**	Lotus	165.344	1'12"039
7.	**Alex Caffi**	Bms Dallara	165.042	1'24"225
8.	**Emanuele Pirro**	Benetton	164.941	1 lap
9.	**Jean Alesi**	Tyrrell	164.087	1 lap
10.	**Derek Warwick**	Arrows	163.708	1 lap
11.	**Stefano Modena**	Brabham	163.316	1 lap
12.	**Martin Brundle**	Brabham	161.382	2 laps
13.	**Jonathan Palmer**	Tyrrell	162.161	4 laps

BEST LAPS

DRIVER AND CAR	LAP	TIME	AVERAGE
Mansell (Ferrari)	66	1'22"637	172.818
Prost (McLaren)	65	1'22"654	172.783
Modena (Brabham)	52	1'23"149	171.754
Berger (Ferrari)	37	1'23"214	171.620
Senna (McLaren)	64	1'23"313	171.416
Boutsen (Williams)	48	1'23"396	171.246
Brundle (Brabham)	39	1'23"442	171.151
Piquet (Lotus)	42	1'23"620	170.787
Nannini (Benetton)	45	1'23"702	170.620
Capelli (Leyton)	19	1'23"710	170.603
Cheever (Arrows)	51	1'23"894	170.229
Caffi (Bms Dallara)	40	1'24"075	169.863
Palmer (Tyrrell)	61	1'24"166	169.679
Warwick (Arrows)	57	1'24"197	169.616
Pirro (Benetton)	65	1'24"305	169.399
Johansson (Onyx)	39	1'24"464	169.080
Patrese (Williams)	43	1'24"559	168.890
Gugelmin (Leyton)	15	1'24"664	168.681
Alesi (Tyrrell)	5	1'24"741	168.528
Nakajima (Lotus)	21	1'24"903	168.206
Gachot (Onyx)	34	1'25"207	167.606
Sala (Minardi)	52	1'26"185	165.704
Martini (Minardi)	15	1'26"691	164.737
Ghinzani (Osella)	17	1'27"012	164.129
Alboreto (Lola)	24	1'27"840	162.582

RETIREMENTS

DRIVER	CAR	LAPS	REASON
Andrea De Cesaris	Bms Dallara	0	Clutch
Pier Luigi Martini	Minardi	19	Universal joint
Piercarlo Ghinzani	Osella	20	Electrical system
Michele Alboreto	Lola	26	Engine
Ivan Capelli	Leyton	26	Wheel hub
Mauricio Gugelmin	Leyton	27	Electrical system
Satoru Nakajima	Lotus	33	Accident
Bertrand Gachot	Onyx	38	Gearbox
Alessandro Nannini	Benetton	46	Gear shift
Stefan Johansson	Onyx	48	Gearbox
Riccardo Patrese	Williams	54	Engine
Gerhard Berger	Ferrari	56	Gearbox
Luis Perez Sala	Minardi	57	Accident

G.P. BELGIO

A. Prost
Mc Laren
1'51"463
(224,146)

T. Boutsen
Williams
1'52"786
(221,517)

N. Mansell
Ferrari
1'52"898
(221,297)

S. Modena
Brabham
1'55"642
(216,046)

D. Warwick
Arrows
1'55"864
(215,632)

A. Caffi
Bms Dallara
1'55"892
(215,580)

P.L. Martini
Minardi
1'56"115
(215,166)

J. Herbert
Tyrrell
1'56"248
(214,920)

A. De Cesaris
Bms Dallara
1'56"257
(214,903)

M. Brundle
Brabham
1'56"327
(214,774)

M. Alboreto
Lola
1'56"616
(214,242)

E. Cheever
Arrows
1'56"748
(213,999)

O. Grouillard
Ligier
1'57"027
(213,489)

A. Senna
Mc Laren
1'50"867
(225,351)

G. Berger
Ferrari
1'52"391
(222,295)

R. Patrese
Williams
1'52"875
(221,342)

A. Nannini
Benetton
1'55"075
(217,111)

M. Gugelmin
Leyton
1'55"729
(215,884)

P. Alliot
Lola
1'55"890
(215,584)

E. Pirro
Benetton
1'55"902
(215,561)

S. Johansson
Onyx
1'56"129
(215,140)

R. Arnoux
Ligier
1'56"251
(214,914)

I. Capelli
Leyton
1'56"291
(214,840)

J. Palmer
Tyrrell
1'56"600
(214,271)

B. Gachot
Onyx
1'56"716
(214,058)

L. Perez Sala
Minardi
1'56"957
(213,617)

Not an easy track, it's the kind drivers both love and fear. A driver can really express himself on this track, and it's surprising how much performance he can get out of his car. The end of August is when Belgium gets all kinds of rain, and this keeps the track pretty wet. Furthermore, most of the track cuts through the Ardenne forest, which makes some sections uneven. Moreover, the trees tend to prevent moisture evaporation, and the spray from the cars doesn't disperse; it falls back down onto the roadway. And all of this adds up to road-holding problems.

Local people traditionally say, "Oh, what a shame. It was sunny up until yesterday." But if you talk to people who visit Spa-Francorchamp several times a year, they'll tell you that the weather's alway bad and always wet.

The weather alternated from dry, to rainy, to wet, but Senna put all his opponents in their place in his usual efficient manner. This also included Prost, whom Ayrton considers his strongest adversary, both on and off the track. Senna definitely demonstrated that he had regained the supremacy he had lost in Hungary because of Patrese. Following behind Senna were Prost (0.8 seconds), Berger (1.5 seconds), Boutsen (almost two seconds, and Mansell (over two seconds).

The others lagged much farther behind. Although this is a driver's track, it's the cars that actually bring in the final results, even during the time trials.

On Sunday it was raining hard, and the track was flooded, but it wasn't raining hard enough to call off the race. Senna was in is element.

Happy as a lark, he was off in a cloud of spray and was soon way out in front, while the others timidly made their way through all that water. Prost, naturally, was very unhappy with that wet track, but since he was still able see something, he decided to let Senna have his way while while he tagged along behind and assured himself a 2nd place. It would be his fifth for the season, which was nothing to sneeze at.

Normal visibility with the tiny rear-view mirrors was already insufficient. Under these wet conditions they had become totally useless. Furthermore, the blue "yield" flag was often interpreted as being meant for one's immediate adversary.

Senna, very determined indeed, sometimes almost took advantage of this blue-flag "misinterpretation." Prost had problems trying to pass Cheever, and Mansell was also not having an easy time of it, which created a lot of tension and bad feelings.

So, Senna came in first - as we all knew he would - thus making it his fifth victory of the season. Mansell provided quite a spectacular show in his many dramatic but futile attempts to pass Prost, as Prost jostled expertly to keep him at bay.

The track is very scenic, safe, and very well laid out. Most of its curves are well designed but there are two or three that are quite dangerous. They get a lot of rain in Belgium and this is a bit of a drawback because the track gets pretty treacherous when it's wet.

I've got a lot of pleasant memories about this track. In 1975 I made the pole position with a Ferrari. It was a great race and I fought it out with Elio De Angelis and Prost for the world championship. In 1988 I was in 3rd place two laps from the finish when my engine quit. In 1987 I would have won that race if I hadn't lost a bearing.

Michele Alboreto

Coached by a certain Ron Dennis in the mid-seventies, Eddie Cheever was already racing professionally when he was only 17.

Besides being a very nice person, during his nine seasons of F1 racing, he has displayed considerable driving skill, sportsmanship, courage and a strong sense of fair play.

One a rainy Sunday in August during the Belgian Grand Prix, Eddie risked losing his "good boy" image.

The accusation was no joke, but Eddie couldn't really take the blame for Mansell only being able to come in 3rd. According to Cesare Fiorio - Ferrari's no-nonsense sports director - if Eddie had let Mansell pass him right away he would have surely come in 2nd, or even 1st!

Fiorio was screaming and hollering all kinds of oaths as he watched "his" Mansell lose precious seconds jostling behind Cheever. Lap after lap went by and Mansell was still trying to get past him. Cheever's good on a wet track, and this plus the bad visibility didn't leave many openings for Mansell.

Cesare Fiorio was storming; he even shook his fist at Cheever from behind the pit wall as he flashed past in his Arrows. He demanded sanctions and asked the race director to flag Cheever down (which is like getting the yellow card in soccer).

When the race was over, the "Rommel of the Ferrari" let out some pretty cutting accusations which were altogether unjust for a driver like Cheever who, as everyone knows, believes in being a good sport and always obeying the rules. However, in the traditional post-race interviews, it was Nigel Mansell who thrust his hand out first to shake Eddie's. Mansell said, "I can't tell you how I would have placed if I hadn't lost so much time trying to double Cheever." This brief comment was without any bitterness and, in fact, his tone seemed to indicate he felt such things are to be expected in a Grand Prix event.

Barnard and Berger: two prestigious Formula 1 personalities who are leaving Ferrari this year.

Prost came in for a nice 2nd place after not wanting to start because of the heavy rain.

Michele Alboreto having trouble with his Larousse-Lamborghini.

FINISHING ORDER

	DRIVER	CAR	AVERAGE	DELAY
1.	**Ayrton Senna**	McLaren	181.576	
2.	**Alain Prost**	McLaren	181.537	"304
3.	**Nigel Mansell**	Ferrari	181.521	"824
4.	**Thierry Boutsen**	Williams	179.958	54"418
5.	**Alessandro Nannini**	Benetton	179.535	1'08"805
6.	**Derek Warwick**	Arrows	179.257	1'18"316
7.	**Mauricio Gugelmin**	Leyton	176.428	1 lap
8.	**Stefan Johansson**	Onyx	175.631	1 lap
9.	**Pier Luigi Martini**	Minardi	175.592	1 lap
10.	**Emanuele Pirro**	Benetton	175.487	1 lap
11.	**Andrea De Cesaris**	Bms Dallara	175.227	1 lap
12.	**Ivan Capelli**	Leyton	174.812	1 lap
13.	**Olivier Grouillard**	Ligier	173.582	1 lap
14.	**Jonathan Palmer**	Tyrrell	171.631	2 laps
15.	**Luis Perez Sala**	Minardi	167.471	3 laps
16.	**Philippe Alliot**	Lola	172.813	5 laps

BEST LAPS

DRIVER AND CAR	LAP	TIME	AVERAGE
Prost (McLaren)	44	2'11"571	189.890
Mansell (Ferrari)	44	2'11"736	189.652
Martini (Minardi)	40	2'12"101	189.128
Senna (McLaren)	42	2'12"890	188.005
De Cesaris (Bms Dallara)	32	2'13"176	187.601
Boutsen (Williams)	39	2'13"842	186.668
Warwick (Arrows)	42	2'14"106	186.300
Nannini (Benetton)	43	2'14"399	185.894
Alliot (Lola)	37	2'14"675	185.513
Capelli (Leyton)	37	2'15"701	184.111
Pirro (Benetton)	41	2'15"868	183.884
Cheever (Arrows)	36	2'16"727	182.729
Grouillard (Ligier)	42	2'17"253	182.029
Johansson (Onyx)	42	2'17"294	181.974
Gugelmin (Leyton)	31	2'17"411	181.820
Patrese (Williams)	16	2'18"273	180.686
Berger (Ferrari)	6	2'18"865	179.916
Gachot (Onyx)	19	2'19"405	179.219
Palmer (Tyrrell)	40	2'19"772	178.748
Alboreto (Lola)	18	2'21"323	176.787
Sala (Minardi)	39	2'22"222	175.669
Caffi (Bms Dallara)	12	2'22"790	174.970
Herbert (Tyrrell)	3	2'26"020	171.100
Arnoux (Ligier)	3	2'26"022	171.098
Brundle (Brabham)	5	2'27"325	169.584
Modena (Brabham)	3	2'31"976	164.394

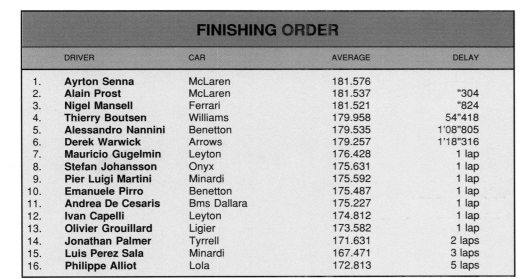

RETIREMENTS

DRIVER	CAR	LAPS	REASON
Johnny Herbert	Tyrrell	3	Accident
René Arnoux	Ligier	4	Accident
Stefano Modena	Brabham	9	Riding alignment
Gerhard Berger	Ferrari	9	Spin
Martin Brundle	Brabham	12	Brakes
Alex Caffi	Bms Dallara	13	Spin
Michele Alboreto	Lola	19	Accident
Riccardo Patrese	Williams	20	Accident
Bertrand Gachot	Onyx	21	Accident
Eddie Cheever	Arrows	38	Wheel loss

G.P. ITALIA

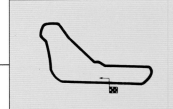

G. Berger
Ferrari
1'24"734
(246,418)

A. Prost
Mc Laren
1'25"510
(244,182)

T. Boutsen
Williams
1'26"155
(242,354)

A. Nannini
Benetton
1'27"052
(239,857)

J. Alesi
(Tyrrell)
1'27"399
(238,904)

M. Brundle
Brabham
1'27"627
(238,283)

J. Palmer
Tyrrell
1'27"822
(237,754)

D. Warwick
Arrows
1'28"092
(237,025)

I. Capelli
Leyton
1'28"430
(236,119)

A. Caffi
Bms Dallara
1'28"596
(235,677)

B. Gachot
Onyx
1'28"684
(235,443)

N. Larini
Osella
1'28"773
(235,207)

L. Perez Sala
Minardi
1'29"293
(233,837)

A. Senna
Mc Laren
1'23"720
(249,403)

N. Mansell
Ferrari
1'24"739
(246,404)

R. Patrese
Williams
1'25"545
(244,082)

P. Alliot
Lola
1'26"985
(240,041)

E. Pirro
Benetton
1'27"397
(238,910)

N. Piquet
Lotus
1'27"508
(238,607)

M. Alboreto
Lola
1'27"803
(237,805)

P.L. Martini
Minardi
1'27"923
(237,481)

A. De Cesaris
Bms Dallara
1'28"129
(236,925)

S. Nakajima
Lotus
1'28"441
(236,090)

O. Grouillard
Ligier
1'28"669
(235,483)

R. Arnoux
Ligier
1'28"669
(235,483)

M. Gugelmin
Leyton
1'28"923
(233,837)

The situation had to be re-evaluated because of the points the two McLaren drivers had that they were fighting out so bitterly for the title.

Prost came to Monza with 62 points to his credit, 11 more than Senna. Mansell had 38. Although the five remaining races to the end of the season, Monza included, could mathematically cause Prost and Senna some concern, no one really believes it does.

Prost had no intention of letting up and was really pouring it on. Besides, with Aryton just one length behind and breathing down his neck, he was getting a little nervous.

In addition, it was already confirmed that Prost would be Mansell's teammate at Ferrari in 1990, with Patrese moving over to the Williams-Renault stable as Boutsen's teammate. The top teams were already set for 1990, except for Benneton, where Piquet's name keeps coming up.

At Monza, the Ferrari wanted to perform well, both in the trials and in the race. They didn't expect to have another lucky break like they had in 1988. They wanted a field victory. Mansell had his steam up, while Berger was really fit to be tied with his eleven drop-outs in eleven races. His confidence in the car was almost completely shot.

The Fiat big-wigs were all present at Monza, including Agnelli, Romiti and Montezemolo. It looked like Berger and Mansell were actually going to do the big number; they were 1st and 2nd on Friday, and in the first two slots five laps from the end of the race.

But mean ol' Senna wasn't going to give anything away to anybody, and really poured it on. What fantastic time: 1 min 23.7 sec, 1 sec better than Berger his future teammate. That was an average of just about 250 km/h on a track with three slow-down chicanes, two of them pretty slow ones.

A race refected the performance in the time trials, except that it took a bit of doing for Prost to get by the Ferraris. Of course, nobody could catch up with Senna.

Mansell's transmission broke down and that finished him. Prost kept a close eye on Berger because he looked as if he had every intention of breaking his no-score jinx. Senna gets out in front and definitely leaves them behind. It looked like it was in the bag for him, but then he had his share of bad luck. Just nine laps from the end of the race, his engine goes on the blink, and that was it for him. Before his engine quit, he was having oil-pressure problems, and wasn't completely caught by surprise. So, it was a "haw-haw" for Senna and another gift for Prost, because he could have caught up with Senna, the way he was driving. By now Prost was really getting close enough to smell that world crown, what with all the points he had accumulated. For a change, Berger had something to be happy about with this race. The two Williams-Renaults came in 3rd and 4th and they weren't complaining either. However, they're looking forward to getting that new FW13 engine, which is supposed to be ready for the Portugal event.

The situation looks critical for Senna. We again have a 20-point difference, and there are only four more races left.

This is the track on which I won most of my early races. So you can understand how dear it is to my heart.

Each time I roll out on this track I'm practically overcome with emotion, my deep-rooted enthusiasm, because for me this is the most beautiful track in the world.

This is the fastest track in the world championship, and if you want to get good results you have to have the right balance between a car's aerodynamic and mechanical characteristics. Actually, the Silverstone track is faster but it's a short track and doesn't have any curves, in the real sense, as we have here at Monza.

You have to keep that pedal pressed all the way down to the floorboard and this is what really pleases race drivers.

Nicola Larini

Could anyone be more lost-looking than Ayrton Senna as he sits there on the guardrail with that blank expression on his face? He still can't get over how he ever lost that race when he had it all sewed up.

Mr. Aryton Senna Da Silva thought he had it all figured out, that it was going to be a triumphal week-end for him. On Saturday, to Mr. Agnelli's consternation, he blithely made off with the pole position; and in the race the following day, with equal blitheness, he took over completely, or so it seemed. He was really banking on winning those 9 points that would have brought him that much closer to his archrival and teammate, Alain Prost, and would have given him the signal that it was going to be tough to keep him down.

Too bad for Ayrton, but that wasn't the way it worked out. Just a few laps from the end of the race, the fates would have it otehwise, and Ayrton's engine went down for the count, taking him down with it.

There was no question about Ayrton's mixed feelings about Monza. He was convinced it was hexed. Already back in 1987, when he was racing for Lotus, he scuttled his last hopes of being in the running along with Piquet for the world's title when he tried doubling Ghinzani on the parabolic and skidded off into the sand. This left him with no choice but to accept a nonsensical 2nd place and cede the championship to Piquet.

That next year, when he was (finally) driving for McLaren, he tried to lap (for the 2nd time) Jean-Louis Schlesser - who replaced the unlucky Mansell in the Williams - and wound up tangling with him. This shelved him two laps before the end, thus leaving the field wide open for Ferrari to score an unexpected double victory. This kind of an accident would ordinarily not have kept him from winning the world title, but in this particular case, the consequences proved a lot more serious and he wound up with a very tough row to hoe.

The ever-vigilant CEA, whose interventations have been truly remarkable.

Prost announces his agreement with Ferrari, and this to be the new 1990 "Cavallino" couple.

The "Goodyear", a tough chicane.

FINISHING ORDER

	DRIVER	CAR	AVERAGE	DELAY
1.	**Alain Prost**	McLaren	232.119	
2.	**Gerhard Berger**	Ferrari	231.763	7"326
3.	**Thierry Boutsen**	Williams	231.392	14"975
4.	**Riccardo Patrese**	Williams	230.249	38"722
5.	**Jean Alesi**	Tyrrell	227.094	1 lap
6.	**Martin Brundle**	Brabham	226.380	1 lap
7.	**Pier Luigi Martini**	Minardi	224.141	1 lap
8.	**Luis Perez Sala**	Minardi	222.938	2 laps
9.	**René Arnoux**	Ligier	221.405	2 laps
10.	**Satoru Nakajima**	Lotus	216.933	2 laps
11.	**Alex Caffi**	Bms Dallara	225.117	6 laps

BEST LAPS

DRIVER AND CAR	LAP	TIME	AVERAGE
Prost (McLaren)	43	1'28"107	236.985
Senna (McLaren)	43	1'28"179	236.791
Boutsen (Williams)	43	1'28"245	236.614
Berger (Ferrari)	43	1'28"712	235.368
Mansell (Ferrari)	33	1'28"820	235.082
Patrese (Williams)	33	1'28"857	234.984
Nannini (Benetton)	27	1'29"726	232.708
Capelli (Leyton)	9	1'30"236	231.393
Brundle (Brabham)	32	1'30"437	230.879
Alesi (Tyrrell)	32	1'30"588	230.494
Piquet (Lotus)	8	1'30"976	229.511
Caffi (Bms Dallara)	42	1'31"112	229.168
De Cesaris (Bms Dallara)	38	1'31"138	229.103
Martini (Minardi)	37	1'31"468	228.277
Sala (Minardi)	41	1'31"535	228.109
Grouillard (Ligier)	29	1'31"639	227.851
Nakajima (Lotus)	42	1'31"931	227.127
Warwick (Arrows)	12	1'32"303	226.211
Larini (Osella)	7	1'32"416	225.935
Palmer (Tyrrell)	12	1'32"474	225.793
Alboreto (Lola)	13	1'32"548	225.613
Arnoux (Ligier)	6	1'32"577	225.542
Gachot (Onyx)	15	1'32"691	225.265
Gugelmin (Leyton)	9	1'33"571	223.146
Alliot (Lola)	1	1'44"035	200.702

RETIREMENTS

DRIVER	CAR	LAPS	REASON
Emanuele Pirro	Benetton	0	Transmission
Philippe Alliot	Lola	1	Accelerator cable
Mauricio Gugelmin	Leyton	14	Riding alignment
Michele Alboreto	Lola	14	Electrical system
Nicola Larini	Osella	16	Gearbox
Derek Warwick	Arrows	18	Engine
Jonathan Palmer	Tyrrell	18	Engine
Nelson Piquet	Lotus	23	Off track
Olivier Grouillard	Ligier	30	Engine
Ivan Capelli	Leyton	30	Engine
Alessandro Nannini	Benetton	33	Brakes
Bertrand Gachot	Onyx	38	Radiator
Nigel Mansell	Ferrari	41	Gearbox
Ayrton Senna	McLaren	44	Engine
Andrea De Cesaris	Bms Dallara	45	Engine

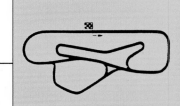

G. Berger
Ferrari
1'16"059
(205.893)

A. Prost
McLaren
1'16"204
(205.501)

R. Patrese
Williams
1'17"281
(202.637)

T. Boutsen
Williams
1'17"801
(201.283)

M. Brundle
Brabham
1'17"874
(201.094)

S. Johansson
Onyx
1'18"105
(200.499)

M. Gugelmin
Leyton
1'18"124
(200.451)

E. Pirro
Benetton
1'18"328
(199.929)

J. Palmer
Tyrrell
1'18"404
(199.735)

N. Piquet
Lotus
1'18"482
(199.536)

D. Warwick
Arrows
1'18"711
(198.956)

I. Capelli
Leyton
1'18"785
(198.769)

E. Cheever
Arrows
1'19"247
(197.610)

A. Senna
McLaren
1'15"468
(207.505)

N. Mansell
Ferrari
1'16"193
(205.531)

P.L. Martini
Minardi
1'16"938
(203.541)

A. Caffi
Bms Dallara
1'17"661
(201.646)

L. Perez Sala
Minardi
1'17"844
(201.172)

S. Modena
Brabham
1'18"093
(200.530)

A. Nannini
Benetton
1'18"115
(200.474)

R. Moreno
Coloni
1'18"196
(200.266)

P. Alliot
Lola
1'18"386
(199.781)

A. De Cesaris
Bms Dallara
1'18"442
(199.638)

M. Alboreto
Lola
1'18"563
(199.330)

R. Arnoux
Ligier
1'18"767
(198.814)

S. Nakajima
Lotus
1'19"165
(197.815)

The Grand Prix's of Portugal and Spain have similar characteristics, and resemble those of Hungary.

You could feel the tension in the air at Portugal. We even went so far as to speculate if Mansell (Ferrari) could possibly be interested in helping Prost (McLaren) - his 1990 teammate - and if the same could apply in the case of Berger (Ferrari) and Senna (McLaren), Berger's 1990 teammate.

Well, as usual, Senna was in the pole position. Berger, still charged up over his 2nd place at Monza, was next to him, raring to go.

Right behind them in the second row was Prost and Mansell, and the natural reaction was to note that the McLaren team was lined up. The big surprise, however, came later with the way the teams with the Pirelli tires performed. Martini, in his Minardi (mounting a "private" engine), gets out in front of Patrese and Boutsen, who debuted the new FW 13.

The Portugal event seemed to have been open to any sort of results. But rather than for the final placings, this Grand Prix will go down in history for its Mansell-Senna-Balestre-black-flag misdeed. After a bit of early hesitation involving Mansell, Berger won in grand style, and Prost copped his sixth 2nd place of the season. Incredibly, Johansson in his Onyx came in 3rd! On the final podium, therefore, we had the fantastic past, present and future representation of the Ferrari team: Johannsson, Berger and Prost.

Getting back to the tire-changing episode. Mansell barrels into the pit at 300 km/h! Overshooting it, he backs the car up, using his engine. Tsk, tsk, he shouldn't have done that: against the rules. Back out on the track he gets the black flag but that doesn't faze him and goes three more laps with the flag still out there. He catches up with Senna, who is four seconds behind Berger, and tries to pass him. They tangle and the two ultra-competitive drivers get lost in the dust off the track, which was a true loss for Senna, because Mansell had already been disqualified. Later, Mansell said he never even saw the black flag, but no one believes him. Heated arguments build up steam until there are insults galore between the two teams.

Final result: Mansell was fined and barred from participating in the next race at Jerez, Spain. Ferrari contested both the fine and the sentencing procedure.

Meanwhile, Prost now had 75 points - not counting his 5th place in Mexico, as provided for by the rules - and Senna only had 51 points.

The Brazilian now found himself in a critical position.

It's a very tough track from every point of view, be it psychological or physical.
Why is this track so tough psychologically? Well, I'll tell you. Right from the start you know you've got 71 laps ahead of you and that kind of weighs on your mind all the way through the race. But notwithstanding all of this physical and psychological torture, I got the best result of my whole Formula 1 career right on this track: a 2nd place. You can well imagine how proud I am about having been able to place 2nd on a track of this type.

Ivan Capelli

Although Ron Dennis is admired today for his superb intelligence, great organizational talents, and keen business sense, when he started out he was a complete unknown.

In fact, in the mid-seventies he was just a mechanic, albeit a good one, who had his eye on better things. Of course, he had a tough road ahead of him, but his rise to success was surprisingly fast. In the very early '80s, with Marlboro's backing, he bought out McLaren, which looked like it was on the skids after having seen better and more glorious days with Emerson Fittipaldi and James Hunt.

In short, Ron Dennis turned McLaren into a model stable and exemplified how a auto-racing team should be managed. Ron had the acumen for finding the best financial partners and engineers, as well as the best drivers.

Such outstanding success, of course, causes many people to be envious, and more than just a few occasions, people would turn up their noses and remark that Ron Dennis was arrogant and outspoken, and the news media did little to improve this rather distasteful image. Actually, most of what was said was unfortunely true.

However, during that Grand Prix at Estoril that had turned out to look more like a bullfight than an auto race, Ron Dennis gave the whole Ferrari clan a lesson on how to behave. There was a awful lot of tension because of Mansell's refusal to leave the track after having been given the black flag and his subsequent accident with Senna, which caused some rather coarse behavior that was certainly not in good taste, nor even tolerable for that matter.

But Ron Dennis kept his cool while the others of his camp shook their heads and said what a pity it was that the Ferrari people didn't match the class of their automobiles. Once upon a time - as many of us remember - things were different; "Ferrari" was synonymous with "gentlemanly sportsmanship." Ah, but unfortunately, times change, and so do proprietors.

The 1989 Grand Prix at Estoril will be remembered for Berger's first victory of the season, but also because of the black flag that was not seen and the Senna-Mansel accident. Johansson and Martini were also among the first to cross the finish line. The Williams was knocked out by radiator problems.

FINISHING ORDER

	DRIVER	CAR	AVERAGE	DELAY
1.	Gerhard Berger	Ferrari	191.418	-
2.	Alain Prost	McLaren	190.348	32"637
3.	Stefan Johansson	Onyx	189.612	55"325
4.	Alessandro Nannini	Benetton	188.741	1'22"369
5.	Pier Luigi Martini	Minardi	188.533	1 lap
6.	Jonathan Palmer	Tyrrell	187.840	1 lap
7.	Satoru Nakajima	Lotus	186.788	1 lap
8.	Martin Brundle	Brabham	186.471	1 lap
9.	Philippe Alliot	Lola	186.463	1 lap
10.	Mauricio Gugelmin	Leyton	185.636	2 laps
11.	Michele Alboreto	Lola	184.600	2 laps
12.	Luis Perez Sala	Minardi	183.934	2 laps
13.	René Arnoux	Ligier	183.808	2 laps
14.	Stefano Modena	Brabham	183.777	2 laps

RETIREMENTS

DRIVER	CAR	LAPS	REASON
Roberto Moreno	Coloni	11	Computer
Andrea De Cesaris	Bms Dallara	17	Engine
Eddie Cheever	Arrows	24	Electrical system
Ivan Capelli	Leyton	25	Computer
Emanuele Pirro	Benetton	29	Riding alignment
Alex Caffi	Bms Dallara	33	Accident
Nelson Piquet	Lotus	33	Accident
Derek Warwick	Arrows	37	Accident
Nigel Mansell	Ferrari	48	Accident
Ayrton Senna	McLaren	48	Accident
Thierry Boutsen	Williams	60	Radiator
Riccardo Patrese	Williams	60	Radiator

BEST LAPS

DRIVER AND CAR	LAP	TIME	AVERAGE
Berger (Ferrari)	49	1'18"986	198.263
Mansell (Ferrari)	44	1'19"047	198.110
Prost (McLaren)	48	1'19"385	197.266
Senna (McLaren)	47	1'19"490	197.006
Boutsen (Williams)	38	1'19"575	196.795
Patrese (Williams)	46	1'19"796	196.250
Gugelmin (Leyton)	69	1'20"571	194.363
Alliot (Lola)	33	1'20"697	194.059
Nannini (Benetton)	43	1'20"722	193.999
Brundle (Brabham)	50	1'21"167	192.936
Martini (Minardi)	34	1'21"170	192.928
Johansson (Onyx)	45	1'21"224	192.800
Caffi (Bms Dallara)	33	1'21"300	192.620
Palmer (Tyrrell)	34	1'21"562	192.001
Arnoux (Ligier)	63	1'21"603	191.905
Alboreto (Lola)	56	1'21"756	191.546
Nakajima (Lotus)	39	1'21"794	191.457
Sala (Minardi)	60	1'22"114	190.710
Piquet (Lotus)	22	1'22"356	190.150
Capelli (Leyton)	18	1'22"873	188.964
Warwich (Arrows)	27	1'22"926	188.843
De Cesaris (Bms Dallara)	4	1'23"592	187.339
Cheever (Arrows)	7	1'23"732	187.025
Pirro (Benetton)	3	1'24"080	186.251
Modena (Brabham)	64	1'24"451	185.433
Moreno (Coloni)	10	1'25"411	183.349

G.P. SPAGNA

G. Berger
Ferrari
1'20"565
(188.479)

A. Senna
McLaren
1'20"291
(189.122)

P.L. Martini
Minardi
1'21"479
(186.365)

A. Prost
McLaren
1'21"368
(186.619)

R. Patrese
Williams
1'21"777
(185.685)

P. Alliot
Lola
1'21"708
(185.842)

M. Brundle
Brabham
1'22"133
(184.881)

N. Piquet
Lotus
1'21"922
(185.357)

E. Pirro
Benetton
1'22"567
(183.909)

J. Alesi
Tyrrell
1'22"363
(184.364)

S. Modena
Brabham
1'22"826
(183.334)

N. Larini
Osella
1'22"620
(183.791)

A. Nannini
Benetton
1'23"105
(182.718)

J. Palmer
Tyrrell
1'23"052
(182.835)

D. Warwick
Arrows
1'23"222
(182.461)

A. De Cesaris
Bms Dallara
1'23"186
(182.540)

S. Nakajima
Lotus
1'23"309
(182.271)

J. Lehto
Onyx
1'23"243
(182.415)

L. Perez Sala
Minardi
1'23"443
(181.978)

I. Capelli
Leyton
1'23"401
(182.070)

E. Cheever
Arrows
1'23"729
(181.357)

T. Boutsen
Williams
1'23"657
(181.513)

O. Grouillard
Ligier
(1'23"931
(180.920)

A. Caffi
Bms Dallara
1'23"763
(181.283)

M. Gugelmin
Leyton
1'24"707
(179.263)

P. Ghinzani
Osella
1'24"003
(180.765)

There's never been so much bad blood over a Formula 1 event as this one. Everybody was nervous, and the drivers were completely ignoring each other. There were even more hard feelings here than there were in Mexico that time when Lorenzo Bandini bumped into Graham Hill, put him out of the race, and let Surtees win the world title for Ferrari. Nigel Mansell wasn't in this race here in Spain, because Balestre had disqualified him. Ferrari put up a fuss because they didn't agree with Balestre's basis for disqualifying him.

The Jerez track is a new one - something like the one in Hungary - and it was too bad that the whole Ferrari team wasn't there.

Senna was on the warpath, and while Berger naturally respected him, he was in no mood to let him get away with anything, least of all a victory, if he was any way near it himself.

The teams with the Pirelli tires also continued to do well in this race. However, it was incredible how well Pierluigi Martini performed in the trials. He was actually in the top-driver class: the ones fighting it out for the world title. The Minardi No. 23 is, in fact, well up there in the official trials classifications, and is also a point of reference for the others. Martini looks like Senna when he's at his best. He wound up the 4th best time and was placed in the 2nd row in the starting line-up, behind Senna, Berger and Prost and well ahead of all the others.

The Williams FW 13 made a very good showing in Portugal, but it was having some tough going here in Spain. Boutsen in

the FW 13 came in 21st, while Patrese - behind the wheel of the old FW12 C - proudly came in 6th.

Alliot's Larousse-Lamborghini was also up there near the front rows, while Alboreto didn't qualify.

The race itself became almost of secondary importance in the light of the polemics, the rivalry between Senna and Prost, and Mansell's absence. The Brazilian breezed along without a care in the world and Berger wasn't able to give him any trouble at all, right from the start. Senna's top-performing McLaren-Honda outclassed them all.

The Senna-Berger tandem twosome, with Prost playing Senna's 2nd handmaiden, led the rest of them all through the race. Prost couldn't figure out if his problem was the car or the way he was managing it. In the end he had make do with a 3rd place and the relative four points that would obligate Senna to win the last two races: the one in Japan and the one in Australia. If Senna can't do this, Prost will win the 3rd world champtionship title of his career. We mustn't forget Ferrari's appeal after Mansell's exclusion from the race. If this appeal is accepted, the results of this Grand Prix could be invalidated, and this would give Prost the title. It's a very serious decision to make, because such factors as the battles that go on out on the track, and the risks the drivers face out there with each and every curve, especially when the title's at stake, have to be taken into consideration. Just think, we still have two to go, the results of which could have no effect on the final result for the year. The world championships have never known such an anomalous situation.

This isn't one of my favorite tracks.
First of all it's always hot there at Jerez, the track's always very dirty, and it's a difficult track. I have a tough time getting used to their way of living over there in that country. For example, the restaurants don't open until 9 in the evening. So I can't enjoy any of their fine food because I have go to bed early.
Now, here's another funny thing. When we have the Grand Prix there, it's wine-making time. And with the mile after mile of vineyards and wineries in the area, the air is always thick with the smell of wine.
We also go to Jerez in the wintertime to run tests, and it's much nicer then because the heat's much more bearable.
These are the reasons I find the G.P. at Jerez so difficult.

Maurizio Gugelmin

No driver has ever been on record as having been disqualified as would be a soccer player, at least until Nigel Mansell came along. As you might remember the Estoril affair prompted the International Commission to bar Nigel from the following Grand Prix event in Spain. But to be more precise, there really was another similar case that happened some years ago (back in 1978) when a very young man from Padoa by the name of Riccardo Patrese was summarily punished by a "kangaroo court" consisting of three of his old-guard "peers".

This completely illegal 3-man "Grand Jury" - consisting of Andretti, Hunt and Lauda - decided that Patrese was responsible for the Monza accident that took the life of Ronnie Peterson, and passed "sentence" that he be barred from the following Grand Prix event in the U.S.A.

Back in 1978, such as decision would presumably have been up to the CSI (the International Sports Commission), headed by a very distinguished Belgian gentleman by the name of Pierre Ugeux, but that's now ancient history.

Nigel's case is quite different because the Federation's whole disqualification procedure was highly debatable; and many people believed Nigel had received unfair treatment, and others even thought he'd been victimized.

The Spanish race didn't turn out to be such a great event, partly because of Mansell's absence. But quite a bit of this strange "pall" that rather hung over the event was also due to a certain concern on the part of the drivers: they realized they had to cut out the fancy stuff or risk getting the "Mansell Treatment". This was probably a good thing, too, because they had been really a bit too much horseplay in the past, and the racing needed to be cleaner and more sportsmanlike. Of course, the public obviously missed the sparkle that Mansell usually gave a race in his determination to overcome any situations of possible inferiority and make as good a showing as possible. Apart from all other considerations, Nigel Mansell's having been barred from the Spanish Grand Prix did make one thing clear: breaking of the Formula 1 rules will no longer be tolerated.

It's Ayrton Senna leading once again, with Berger trying (in vain) to catch up with him, and Prost's 3rd spot not seriously threatened by Philippe Alliot in his Lola Larousse (which uses Mauro Forghieri's Lamborghini engine).

FINISHING ORDER

	DRIVER	CAR	AVERAGE	DELAY
1.	**Ayrton Senna**	McLaren	171.374	-
2.	**Gerhard Berger**	Ferrari	170.660	27"051
3.	**Alain Prost**	McLaren	169.960	53"788
4.	**Jean Alesi**	Tyrrell	169.017	1 lap
5.	**Riccardo Patrese**	Williams	169.013	1 lap
6.	**Philippe Alliot**	Lola	167.646	1 lap
7.	**Andrea De Cesaris**	Bms Dallara	167.318	1 lap
8.	**Nelson Piquet**	Lotus	166.563	2 laps
9.	**Derek Warwick**	Arrows	166.298	2 laps
10.	**Jonathan Palmer**	Tyrrell	164.842	2 laps

RETIREMENTS

DRIVER	CAR	LAPS	REASON
Satoru Nakajima	Lotus	0	Off track
Nicola Larini	Osella	6	Off track
Stefano Modena	Brabham	11	Engine
Alessandro Nannini	Benetton	14	Spin
Piercarlo Ghinzani	Osella	17	Gearbox
Jarvi Lehto	Onyx	20	Gearbox
Ivan Capelli	Leyton	23	Transmission
Pier Luigi Martini	Minardi	27	Off track
Olivier Grouillard	Ligier	34	Engine
Thierry Boutsen	Williams	40	Fuel pump
Luis Perez Sala	Minardi	47	Injection system
Mauricio Gugelmin	Leyton	47	Injection system
Martin Brundle	Brabham	51	Off track
Alex Caffi	Bms Dallara	55	Engine
Emanuele Pirro	Benetton	59	Off track
Eddie Cheever	Arrows	61	Engine

BEST LAPS

DRIVER AND CAR	LAP	TIME	AVERAGE
Senna (McLaren)	55	1'25"779	177.022
Patrese (Williams)	71	1'26"211	176.135
Berger (Ferrari)	53	1'26"213	176.131
Alliot (Lola)	32	1'26"272	176.011
Piquet (Lotus)	70	1'26"476	175.596
Cheever (Arrows)	56	1'26"650	175.243
Prost (McLaren)	51	1'26"758	175.025
Alesi (Tyrrell)	38	1'26"807	174.926
Warwick (Arrows)	61	1'27"186	174.166
Pirro (Benetton)	44	1'27"272	173.994
Nannini (Benetton)	14	1'27"301	173.936
Palmer (Tyrrell)	57	1'27"540	173.461
Brundle (Brabham)	41	1'27"870	172.810
De Cesaris (Bms Dallara)	56	1'28"016	172.523
Gugelmin (Leyton)	43	1'28"285	171.998
Sala (Minardi)	45	1'28"322	171.925
Capelli (Leyton)	21	1'28"582	171.421
Martini (Minardi)	3	1'29"00"	170.616
Caffi (Bms Dallara)	23	1'29"338	169.970
Boutsen (Williams)	39	1'29"457	169.744
Grouillard (Ligier)	11	1'29"611	169.452
Modena (Brabham)	11	1'30"142	168.454
Lehto (Onyx Ore)	8	1'30"206	168.335
Larini (Osella)	5	1'30"578	167.643

G.P. GIAPPONE

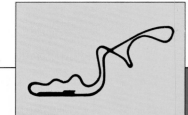

A. Prost
McLaren
1'39"771
(211.408)

N. Mansell
Ferrari
1'40"407
(210.069)

A. Nannini
Benetton
1'41"103
(208.623)

P. Alliot
Lola
1'41"336
(208.143)

N. Larini
Osella
1'41"519
(207.768)

S. Nakajima
Lotus
1'41"988
(206.813)

L. Perez Sala
Minardi
1'42"283
(206.216)

A. De Cesaris
Bms Dallara
1'42"581
(205.617)

J. Alesi
Tyrrell
1'42"709
(205.361)

M. Gugelmin
Leyton
1'42"880
(205.019)

E. Pirro
Benetton
1'43"063
(204.655)

E. Cheever
Arrows
1'43"511
(203.770)

J. Palmer
Tyrrell
1'43"757
(203.287)

A. Senna
McLaren
1'38"041
(215.139)

G. Berger
Ferrari
1'40"187
(210.530)

R. Patrese
Williams
1'40"936
(208.968)

T. Boutsen
Williams
1'41"324
(208.168)

S. Modena
Brabham
1'41"458
(207.893)

N. Piquet
Lotus
1'41"802
(207.190)

M. Brundle
Brabham
1'42"182
(206.420)

A. Caffi
Bms Dallara
1'42"488
(205.804)

I. Capelli
Leyton
1'42"672
(205.435)

P. Barilla
Minardi
1'42"780
(205.219)

B. Schneider
Zakspeed
1'42"892
(204.996)

O. Grouillard
Ligier
1'43"379
(204.030)

D. Warwick
Arrows
1'43"599
(203.597)

The theater for this Grand Prix event was the Suzuka track, where both Honda and McLaren test their vehicles. The first thing everybody heard upon arrival was that Ferrari had announced - very sportsmanlike - that it would not appeal against Mansell's disqualification. This was a very wise move because not only would it have com promised the sports results of the two McLaren-Honda drivers, but it would also have certainly tarnished Ferrari's image. It was also rumored that Ferrari's decision had some political basis. It was believed Ferrari and Balestre had decided to refrain from starting the polemics because it could have dragged onward and turned into a sort of feud between the two teams.

Well, that having been settled, the Suzuka trials had the same old clich{: Senna's results were astonishing, and Prost was behind him and followed by the Ferrari, Benetton and Williams-Renault.

The outcome of this race seemed to depend on the amount of grit, race-management capability, and vehicle reliability. Senna and Prost were in the first row, and all things were equal, except for their individual experience, and neither of them had any interest in placing 2nd.

If Senna were to win, it would give him a chance to win again in Australia. As far as Prost was concerned, if Senna

were to win, his results would only have statistical value. The Frenchman, however, knew that he had to go for broke, even if it meant risking some mechanical failure and dropping out. As a sidelight, Martini's rib problem permitted Barilla to make his debut with Minardi.

With all eyes on Senna and Prost in the first row, it seemed everybody was taking Senna's superiority for granted. But at the green light, Prost was off like a scared rabbit, and at the end of the first lap, has more than a second lead over Senna.

It looked like the usual race except that Senna and Prost had changed positions. Now it was Senna who was trying to catch up with Prost.

This highly unusual situation stole the thunder from all the others, and hardly anybody actually noticed (or really cared) that Nannini was in third position, that the two Tyrrells had dropped out, and that Patrese and Boutsen in their Williams-Renaults were in the fourth and fifth positions, respectively. Senna was slow when accelerating, but made up for it on the curves, fast straightaways, and when having to brake. But he'd lose to Prost and even to cars he was lapping when coming out of large bends and curves. Even Senna was slower than Prost, but he picked up lost time on the wide curves and braking places.

What makes Japan so fascinating is that it's so completely different from Europe or America. Their culture's different, they have a different life-style and their food is different.

That Japanese track is about as beautiful a track you'll find anywhere, but it's also one of the most difficult. The thing that bothers me the most about Japan is that I can't eat anything. Their food is just too different from ours, and this gets to be a real problem.

Suzuka is where the Honda plant is located, and the track there really lets you pull out all the stops.

Eddie Cheever

From the early days of his appearance in the F1, Alessandro Nannini made a hit with everybody, and a lot of people were certain he would make a big name for himself in Formula 1 racing.

In fact, after his first two years with Minardi, he was asked to join the more competitive Benetton team where he got the chance to prove that his success was due to his talent and not to the fact that he was the brother of rock star, Gianna Nannini.

He was able to score points several times but would have been able to win one or more races if he had a more competitive car.

A typically witty, wisecracking Tuscan, Alessandro didn't appear to take his rather mediocre luck very hard, but deep down it was eating him up. Formula 1 history is full of examples of drivers who were never able to win a race, but Alessandro was risking getting a complex over his frustration.

His big day finally came in the Japanese Grand Prix. What seemed like the usual duel between Senna and Prost for first place suddenly took an unexpected turn. The two McLarens got tangled up and they both wound up out of the race. Nannini took over the lead. Then Senna got back into the race and made a spectacular comeback and cut the finish line before Nannini in his Benetton.

But then the big surprise! Senna was disqualified, leaving his prestigious top podium position to Nannini, who was frankly quite incredulous over the whole thing. Nannini ran a very good race, but everyone knew - and no one better than he that his victory had been an out-and-out gift from Lady Luck.

Nothwithstanding this luck-assisted victory, just having been able to win did great things both for his morale and his self-confidence.

Finally - after all that tension - even the wives get up onto the podium along with the three winners. Senna's disqualification gave Nannini the victory, will the two Williams in 2nd and 3rd place.

FINISHING ORDER

	DRIVER	CAR	AVERAGE	DELAY
1.	**Alessandro Nannini**	Benetton	195.907	
2.	**Riccardo Patrese**	Williams	195.499	11"904
3.	**Thierry Boutsen**	Williams	195.446	13"446
4.	**Nelson Piquet**	Lotus	192.393	1'44"225
5.	**Martin Brundle**	Brabham	192.118	1 lap
6.	**Derek Warwick**	Arrows	191.779	1 lap
7.	**Mauricio Gugelmin**	Leyton	191.173	1 lap
8.	**Eddie Cheever**	Arrows	190.019	1 lap
9.	**Alex Caffi**	Bms Dallara	188.583	1 lap
10.	**Andrea De Cesaris**	Bms Dallara	188.438	2 laps

RETIREMENTS

DRIVER	CAR	LAPS	REASON
Paolo Barilla	Minardi	0	Not classified
Luis Perez Sala	Minardi	0	Not classified
Bernd Schneider	Zakspeed	1	Transmission
Jonathan Palmer	Tyrrell	20	Fuel loss
Nicola Larini	Osella	21	Brakes
Ivan Capelli	Leyton	27	Suspension system
Olivier Grouillard	Ligier	31	Engine
Emanuele Pirro	Benetton	33	Accident
Gerhard Berger	Ferrari	34	Gearbox
Philippe Alliot	Lola	36	Engine
Jean Alesi	Tyrrell	37	Gearbox
Satoru Nakajima	Lotus	41	Engine
Nigel Mansell	Ferrari	43	Engine
Stefano Modena	Brabham	46	Engine
Alain Prost	McLaren	46	Accident

BEST LAPS

DRIVER AND CAR	LAP	TIME	AVERAGE
Prost (McLaren)	43	1'43"506	203.779
Berger (Ferrari)	26	1'44"189	202.443
Nannini (Benetton)	28	1'44"919	201.035
Pirro (Benetton)	25	1'45"049	200.786
Mansell (Ferrari)	32	1'45"077	200.728
Boutsen (Williams)	37	1'45"115	200.660
Patrese (Williams)	26	1'45"335	200.244
Alliot (Lola)	25	1'45"353	200.206
Brundle (Brabham)	46	1'46"194	198.621
De Cesaris (Bms Dallara)	35	1'46"225	198.563
Piquet (Lotus)	33	1'46"420	198.199
Alesi (Tyrrell)	34	1'46"674	197.727
Warwick (Arrows)	32	1'47"069	196.998
Nakajima (Lotus)	30	1'47"338	196.504
Capelli (Leyton)	25	1'47"465	196.272
Cheever (Arrows)	27	1'47"920	195.445
Gugelmin (Leyton)	43	1'47"976	195.343
Grouillard (Ligier)	22	1'48"145	195.038
Modena (Brabham)	31	1'48"609	194.204
Caffi (Bms Dallara)	29	1'49"322	192.938
Larini (Osella)	19	1'49"479	192.661
Palmer (Tyrrell)	4	1'49"910	191.906
Schneider (Zakspeed)	1	2'11"970	159.827

G.P. AUSTRALIA

A. Prost
Mc Laren
1'17"403
(175.807)

A. Nannini
Benetton
1'17"762
(174.995)

R. Patrese
Williams
1'17"827
(174.849)

S. Modena
Brabham
1'18"750
(172.800)

A. Caffi
Bms Dallara
1'18"857
(172.566)

M. Brundle
Brabham
1'19"136
(171.957)

G. Berger
Ferrari
1'19"238
(171.736)

I. Capelli
Leyton
1'19"269
(171.669)

N. Piquet
Lotus
1'19"392
(171.403)

D. Warwick
Arrows
1'19"599
(170.957)

E. Cheever
Arrows
1'19"922
(170.266)

O. Grouillard
Ligier
1'20"073
(169.945)

R. Arnoux
Ligier
1'20"391
(169.273)

A. Senna
Mc Laren
1'16"665
(177.500)

P.L. Martini
Minardi
1'17"623
(175.309)

T. Boutsen
Williams
1'17"791
(174.930)

N. Mansell
Ferrari
1'18"313
(173.764)

A. De Cesaris
Bms Dallara
1'18"828
(172.629)

N. Larini
Osella
1'19"110
(172.014)

E. Pirro
Benetton
1'19"217
(171.781)

J. Alesi
Tyrrell
1'19"259
(171.690)

J. Lehto
Onyx
1'19"309
(171.582)

P. Alliot
Lola
1'19"568
(171.024)

P. Ghinzani
Osella
1'19"691
(170.760)

S. Nakajima
Lotus
1'20"066
(169.960)

M. Gugelmin
Leyton
1'20"191
(169.695)

When things start off on the wrong foot there's nothing you can do about it. The Australian race already had a dark cloud over its head because of the polemics linked with the Japanese Grand Prix, by the "judicial rulings" passed by the International Federation and by the public statements made by Senna, Prost and Ron Dennis. Instead a being a great final race, with everybody in a festive mood, it turned out to be just another round of polemics, what with the horrible weather, the aborted first start (with cars doing mad spins all over the place), the second start with Prost deciding to sit it out, and the large number of spectacular accidents that involved several top drivers including Senna. The trials in this last act of the '89 season started off well. There was a lot of new blood in the first rows, and this gave the impression that - apart from Senna, who was sure to lead the pack - it was just about an even-Steven go for all the others.

The cars with the Pirelli tires (the Minardi, Dallara, and Brabham) even had a good chance making the podium. The Ferrari was going through a crisis while the Benetton seemed very promising. The car looked like it was streaking along, even when it was standing still. Could it be that Barnard, after just having left Ferrari a short while ago, has been able to create a car that can outperform his Ferrari F1/89? Well, we'll have to wait till next year to get the answer to that one.

The Australian race was the last chance to bring out any such indications before the onset of winter and the winter tests, the post-season comparison between the various teams, and the first 1990 races in March.

That veritable cloudburst that greeted that unlucky event at Adelaide continued uninterruptedly all through the day. The track had a layer of water on it and things got steadily worse and worse. Most of the drivers had been figuring on giving the last race as much as they possibly could, but that track washed away all their hopes of doing anything really decent.

When the track officials decided to let the race start, the track conditions were definitely unsafe and none of the drivers wanted the race to start, except for Senna. It wasn't clear whether he was insisting on going ahead with the race because the world title was still contingent on a legal decision, or because he didn't want to jeopardize his probationary status by opposing the racing authorities' decision.

So, with the track awash like a ship's top deck in a hurricane, they grimly lined up and at the green light were off in one helluva lot of spray. No one could see where they were going, and, of course, all hell broke loose with cars waltzing and spinning around like crazy, or bouncing off the track. It was absolutely mad. Senna was trying to lap another car on the straightaway, didn't see him in time, and crashed right smack bang into him.

Needless to say, they all had to be called back to the starting line. Something over an hour later they were given the go-ahead for the second start. Off they were again with the same problem; the spray was still blinding and it was a miracle how nobody got killed, although there were a large number of accidents. In fact, only eight cars finally made it across the finish line. Boutsen in his Williams came in first (doing a repeat of his performance in Canada), while Nannini came in second. He drove the whole race like he knew he was going to make it, probably inspired by thinking of a great '90 season, and an even greater '91 season with the 12-cylinder Ford engine.

Patrese came in third, and also placed 3rd in the world classifications, after Prost and Senna.

G.P. AUSTRALIA

Australia is my favorite country and where I have the most luck.
In 1981 I raced in Formula Atlantic and won with Allan Jones and Nelson Piquet behind me. There were both F1 and Atlantic drivers in this race.
On this occasion I was able to give Nelson Piquet the satisfaction of knowning that all the faith he had in me was not in vain. I won three Formula Atlantic Grand Prix races, and I won my very first world point almost immediately; I won it in my second G.P.
The fans are enthusiastic and really get into the spirit of racing down there. They really love automobile racing with a passion. And they're especially hospitable to foreigners.
It's a street circuit but you can drive on it like any other normal race track.
I think Australia's the most beautiful place in the world.

Roberto Moreno

melen in his Lola spun off the track, killing four spectators and injuring 6 others.

Niki Lauda also surprised everybody with his sensational refusal to race that very next year in the Japanese Grand Prix, which was held at the foot of Mt. Fuji and was the deciding race for world championship title.   There was a torrential rain that day, and it only took Lauda two laps to be convinced that that kind of racing wasn't for him. Of course, his terrible accident at Nurburgring, where he was so badly burned, was still fresh in his mind, and he'd only decided to race once again to try to defend the title he had won the previous year. This year in Australia, it was Alain Prost who turned chicken when he saw all that water on the track. He hates the hell out of a wet track anyway. However, he had guts enough to try a couple of laps, but when everybody was "waltzing Matida," spinning around like crazy tops, he was more than convinced that he didn't want any part of that madhouse affair. In fact, the race had to have a fresh start, by which time Alain had found himself a nice, dry, cosy spectator's spot in the pits.

Of course, Alain's refusal to race caused a lot of comment. Some were asking if he actually had the right to choose, inasmuch as his being on in the line-up would seem to make it obligatory for him to participate in the race.

These and other debatable points were still the object of argument well after the Australian Grand Prix had ended a season already overly fraught with polemics.

Very few Formula 1 drivers have ever opted out of a Grand Prix event because of poor safety conditions.

The first one that ever did this was Emerson Fittipaldi. This as in 1975, and the race was the Spanish Grand Prix, which was being held, that year, on the city track of Barcelona in Moantjuich park.

This very likeable Brazilian driver, who was the world's champion at the time, was very frank in his opinion. He flatly stated that the Barcelona track was just too damned dangerous. Emerson certainly knew what he was talking about, because during the race Stom-

The nightmare's finally over.
With Thierry Boutsen's victory and
Patrese's 3rd place in what was its most
difficult race of the season, Williams'
success is complete.

FINISHING ORDER

	DRIVER	CAR	AVERAGE	DELAY
1.	**Thierry Boutsen**	Williams	131.981	
2.	**Alessandro Nannini**	Benetton	131.459	28"658
3.	**Riccardo Patrese**	Williams	131.295	37"683
4.	**Satoru Nakajima**	Lotus	131.211	42"331
5.	**Emanuele Pirro**	Benetton	126.344	2 laps
6.	**Pier Luigi Martini**	Minardi	125.270	3 laps
7.	**Mauricio Gugelmin**	Leyton	124.313	4 laps
8.	**Stefano Modena**	Brabham	119.123	6 laps

RETIREMENTS

DRIVER	CAR	LAPS	REASON
Nicola Larini	Osella	0	No start
Alain Prost	McLaren	0	No start
René Arnoux	Ligier	4	Off track
Jean Alesi	Tyrrell	5	Computer
Gerhard Berger	Ferrari	6	Accident
Philippe Alliot	Lola	6	Accident
Derek Warwick	Arrows	7	Off track
Martin Brundle	Brabham	12	Accident
Andrea De Cesaris	Bms Dallara	12	Off track
Ivan Capelli	Leyton	13	Radiator
Alex Caffi	Bms Dallara	13	Off track
Ayrton Senna	McLaren	13	Accident
Nigel Mansell	Ferrari	17	Off track
Piercarlo Ghinzani	Osella	18	Accident
Nelson Piquet	Lotus	19	Accident
Olivier Grouillard	Ligier	22	Off track
Jarvi Lehto	Onyx	27	Engine
Eddie Cheever	Arrows	42	Off track

BEST LAPS

DRIVER AND CAR	LAP	TIME	AVERAGE
Nakajima (Lotus)	64	1'38"480	138.180
Patrese (Williams)	59	1'38"685	137.893
Nannini (Benetton)	59	1'40"336	135.624
Boutsen (Williams)	54	1'40"380	135.565
Senna (McLaren)	6	1'41"159	134.521
Mansell (Ferrari)	16	1'42"406	132.883
Lehto (Onyx)	26	1'42"509	132.749
Pirro (Benetton)	49	1'43"144	131.932
Piquet (Lotus)	19	1'44"277	130.499
Cheever (Arrows)	22	1'44"305	130.464
Gugelmin (Leyton)	62	1'44"734	129.929
Alesi (Tyrrell)	5	1'44"900	129.724
Warwick (Arrows)	6	1'45"700	128.742
Martini (Minardi)	57	1'46"189	128.149
Berger (Ferrari)	6	1'46"911	127.283
Grouillard (Ligier)	19	1'46"973	127.210
Caffi (Bms Dallara)	11	1'47"255	126.875
De Cesaris (Bms Dallara)	10	1'47"525	126.557
Modena (Brabham)	56	1'48"171	125.801
Brundle (Brabham)	9	1'48"366	125.574
Capelli (Leyton)	9	1'48"521	125.395
Alliot (Lola)	6	1'49"251	124.557
Arnoux (Ligier)	3	1'50"375	123.289
Ghinzani (Osella)	16	1'51"975	121.527

1989 - BRAZILIAN GRAND PRIX - RIO DE JANEIRO
OFFICIAL PRACTICE TIMES

POS	NR	DRIVER	NAT	CAR	1st SESSION B.TIME LAP	2nd SESSION B.TIME LAP	km/h DIFF
1	1	A.SENNA	BRA	MARLBORO McLAREN HONDA	1'26.205 4	1'25.302■ 4	212.323
2	6	R.PATRESE	ITA	CANON WILLIAMS RENAULT	1'26.172■ 4	7'12.732 3	0.870
3	28	G.BERGER	AUT	FERRARI	1'26.271 5	1'26.394 6	0.969
4	5	T.BOUTSEN	BEL	CANON WILLIAMS RENAULT	1'27.367 4	1'26.459■ 4	1.157
5	2	A.PROST	FRA	MARLBORO McLAREN HONDA	1'27.095 3	1'26.620■ 4	1.318
6	27	N.MANSELL	GBR	FERRARI	1'27.249 2	1'26.772■ 2	1.470
7	16	I.CAPELLI	ITA	LEYTON HOUSE MARCH JUDD	1'27.525 4	1'27.035■ 5	1.733
8	9	D.WARWICK	GBR	USF&G ARROWS FORD	1'27.937 4	1'27.408■ 6	2.106
9	11	N.PIQUET	BRA	CAMEL LOTUS JUDD	1'28.423 5	1'27.437■ 5	2.135
10	20	J.HERBERT	GBR	BENETTON FORD	1'27.626■ 6	1'27.754 5	2.324
11	19	A.NANNINI	ITA	BENETTON FORD	1'28.394 6	1'27.865■ 6	2.563
12	15	M.GUGELMIN	BRA	LEYTON HOUSE MARCH JUDD	1'27.956■ 4	1'28.581 5	2.654
13	7	M.BRUNDLE	GBR	BRABHAM JUDD	1'29.138 6	1'28.274■ 5	2.972
14	8	S.MODENA	ITA	BRABHAM JUDD	1'28.621■ 7	1'28.942 4	3.319
15	22	A.DE CESARIS	ITA	BMS DALLARA FORD	1'29.005■ 6	1'29.206 6	3.703
16	23	P.MARTINI	ITA	MINARDI FORD	0	1'29.435■ 4	4.133
17	38	C.DANNER	BRD	RIAL FORD	1'30.460 4	1'29.455■ 6	4.153
18	3	J.PALMER	GBR	TYRRELL FORD	1'30.443 4	1'29.573■ 5	4.271
19	17	N.LARINI	ITA	OSELLA FORD	1'31.341 5	1'30.146■ 2	4.844
20	4	M.ALBORETO	ITA	TYRRELL FORD	1'32.260 7	1'30.255■ 4	4.953
21	12	S.NAKAJIMA	JPN	CAMEL LOTUS JUDD	1'30.942 2	1'30.375■ 5	5.073
22	26	O.GROUILLARD	FRA	LIGIER LOTO FORD	1'30.410■ 9	1'30.666 2	5.108
23	24	L.SALA	SPA	MINARDI FORD	1'30.702 4	1'30.643■ 7	5.341
24	10	E.CHEEVER	USA	USF&G ARROWS FORD	1'30.657■ 2	1'31.068 6	5.355
25	34	B.SCHNEIDER	BRD	WEST ZAKSPEED YAMAHA	1'32.346 2	1'30.861■ 3	5.559
26	30	P.ALLIOT	FRA	L.& C. LOLA LAMBORGHINI	1'31.872 9	1'31.009■ 2	5.707
27	29	Y.DALMAS	FRA	L.& C. LOLA LAMBORGHINI	1'32.411 7	1'31.260■ 6	5.958
28	25	R.ARNOUX	FRA	LIGIER LOTO FORD	0	1'31.376■ 6	6.074
29	33	G.FOITEK	SUI	EUROBRUN JUDD	1'31.791■ 4	1'53.570 2	6.489
30	31	R.MORENO	BRA	COLONI FORD	1'32.561■ 7	1'34.894 4	7.259

1989 - KRONENBOURG SAN MARINO GRAND PRIX - IMOLA
OFFICIAL PRACTICE TIMES

POS	NR	DRIVER	NAT	CAR	1st SESSION B.TIME LAP	2nd SESSION B.TIME LAP	km/h DIFF
1	1	A.SENNA	BRA	MARLBORO McLAREN HONDA	1'42.939 18	1'26.010■ 8	210.952
2	2	A.PROST	FRA	MARLBORO McLAREN HONDA	1'44.558 10	1'26.235■15	0.225
3	27	N.MANSELL	GBR	FERRARI	1'49.665 5	1'27.652■17	1.642
4	6	R.PATRESE	ITA	CANON WILLIAMS RENAULT	1'47.486 14	1'27.920■17	1.910
5	28	G.BERGER	AUT	FERRARI	1'42.781 15	1'28.089■11	2.079
6	5	T.BOUTSEN	BEL	CANON WILLIAMS RENAULT	1'49.451 8	1'28.308■21	2.298
7	19	A.NANNINI	ITA	BENETTON FORD	1'45.536 17	1'28.854■15	2.844
8	11	N.PIQUET	BRA	CAMEL LOTUS JUDD	1'48.124 9	1'29.057■19	3.047
9	21	A.CAFFI	ITA	BMS DALLARA FORD	1'48.868 12	1'29.069■ 7	3.059
10	26	O.GROUILLARD	FRA	LIGIER FORD	1'47.371 17	1'29.104■23	3.094
11	23	P.MARTINI	ITA	MINARDI FORD	1'47.321 15	1'29.152■19	3.142
12	9	D.WARWICK	GBR	USF&G ARROWS FORD	1'47.859 13	1'29.281■ 7	3.271
13	16	I.CAPELLI	ITA	LEYTON HOUSE MARCH JUDD	1'48.178 11	1'29.385■ 3	3.375
14	17	N.LARINI	ITA	FONDMETAL OSELLA FORD	1'47.577 7	1'29.488■11	3.478
15	24	L.SALA	SPA	MINARDI FORD	1'46.800 16	1'29.503■21	3.493
16	22	A.DE CESARIS	ITA	BMS DALLARA FORD	1'53.681 4	1'29.669■ 8	3.659
17	8	S.MODENA	ITA	BRABHAM JUDD	1'48.415 16	1'29.761■ 4	3.751
18	40	G.TARQUINI	ITA	AGS FORD	1'48.795 13	1'29.913■17	3.903
19	15	M.GUGELMIN	BRA	LEYTON HOUSE MARCH JUDD	1'52.119 4	1'30.163■15	4.153
20	30	P.ALLIOT	FRA	L.& C. LOLA LAMBORGHINI	2'00.293 2	1'30.168■ 8	4.158
21	10	E.CHEEVER	USA	USF&G ARROWS FORD	1'45.375 19	1'30.233■ 8	4.223
22	7	M.BRUNDLE	GBR	BRABHAM JUDD	1'46.279 10	1'30.271■ 3	4.261
23	20	J.HERBERT	GBR	BENETTON FORD	2'05.126 2	1'30.347■ 9	4.337
24	12	S.NAKAJIMA	JPN	CAMEL LOTUS JUDD	1'46.483 16	1'30.697■10	4.687
25	3	J.PALMER	GBR	TYRRELL FORD	1'51.229 12	1'30.928■ 8	4.918
26	29	Y.DALMAS	FRA	L.& C. LOLA LAMBORGHINI	1'58.083 3	1'31.137■10	5.127
27	4	M.ALBORETO	ITA	TYRRELL FORD	1'51.329 9	1'31.206■12	5.196
28	25	R.ARNOUX	FRA	LIGIER FORD	1'48.091 9	1'31.268■ 9	5.258
29	38	C.DANNER	BRD	RIAL FORD	1'47.967 10	1'31.342■12	5.332
30	31	R.MORENO	BRA	COLONI FORD	1'50.947 6	1'31.775■11	5.765

These statistics have been kindly given by Olivetti's "Servizio Computer per lo Sport"

1989 - MONACO GRAND PRIX - MONTE-CARLO
OFFICIAL PRACTICE TIMES

POS	NR	DRIVER	NAT	TEAM	1st SESSION B.TIME	LAP	2nd SESSION B.TIME	LAP	km/h DIFF
1	1	A.SENNA	BRA	MARLBORO McLAREN HONDA	1'24.126	9	1'22.308■	6	145.561
2	2	A.PROST	FRA	MARLBORO McLAREN HONDA	1'24.671	4	1'23.456■	8	1.148
3	5	T.BOUTSEN	BEL	CANON WILLIAMS RENAULT	1'25.540	7	1'24.332■	7	2.024
4	7	M.BRUNDLE	GBR	BRABHAM JUDD	1'26.970	18	1'24.580■	17	2.272
5	27	N.MANSELL	GBR	FERRARI	1'25.363	10	1'24.735■	12	2.427
6	9	D.WARWICK	GBR	USF&G ARROWS FORD	1'26.606	4	1'24.791■	3	2.483
7	6	R.PATRESE	ITA	CANON WILLIAMS RENAULT	1'27.138	5	1'25.021■	9	2.713
8	8	S.MODENA	ITA	BRABHAM JUDD	1'27.598	7	1'25.086■	6	2.778
9	21	A.CAFFI	ITA	BMS DALLARA FORD	1'27.894	7	1'25.481■	11	3.173
10	22	A.DE CESARIS	ITA	BMS DALLARA FORD	1'26.617	7	1'25.515■	10	3.207
11	23	P.MARTINI	ITA	SCM MINARDI FORD	1'28.469	13	1'26.288■	15	3.980
12	4	M.ALBORETO	ITA	TYRRELL FORD		0	1'26.388■	12	4.080
13	40	G.TARQUINI	ITA	AGS FORD	1'26.603	9	1'26.422■	9	4.114
14	15	M.GUGELMIN	BRA	LEYTON HOUSE MARCH JUDD	1'28.917	8	1'26.522■	7	4.214
15	19	A.NANNINI	ITA	BENETTON FORD	1'28.608	3	1'26.599■	4	4.291
16	26	O.GROUILLARD	FRA	LIGIER LOTO FORD	1'27.040	12	1'26.792■	4	4.484
17	30	P.ALLIOT	FRA	L.& C. LOLA LAMBORGHINI	1'26.975	9	1'26.857■	10	4.549
18	32	P.RAPHANEL	FRA	COLONI FORD	1'30.264	2	1'27.011■	7	4.703
19	11	N.PIQUET	BRA	CAMEL LOTUS JUDD	1'29.047	18	1'27.046■	5	4.738
20	10	E.CHEEVER	USA	USF&G ARROWS FORD	1'28.461	6	1'27.117■	12	4.809
21	25	R.ARNOUX	FRA	LIGIER LOTO FORD	1'30.003	7	1'27.182■	10	4.874
22	16	I.CAPELLI	ITA	LEYTON HOUSE MARCH JUDD	1'29.800	14	1'27.302■	3	4.994
23	3	J.PALMER	GBR	TYRRELL FORD	1'29.151	16	1'27.452■	14	5.144
24	20	J.HERBERT	GBR	BENETTON FORD	1'29.661	4	1'27.706■	12	5.398
25	31	R.MORENO	BRA	COLONI FORD	1'30.209	11	1'27.721■	7	5.413
26	24	L.SALA	SPA	SCM MINARDI FORD	1'28.886	6	1'27.786■	4	5.478
27	38	C.DANNER	BRD	RIAL FORD	1'28.737	7	1'27.910■	9	5.602
28	29	Y.DALMAS	FRA	L.& C. LOLA LAMBORGHINI	1'29.794	8	1'27.946■	3	5.638
29	12	S.NAKAJIMA	JPN	CAMEL LOTUS JUDD	1'28.568	11	1'28.419■	13	6.111

1989 - MEXICAN GRAND PRIX - MEXICO CITY
OFFICIAL PRACTICE TIMES

POS	NR	DRIVER	NAT	CAR	1st SESSION B.TIME	LAP	2nd SESSION B.TIME	LAP	km/h DIFF
1	1	A.SENNA	BRA	MARLBORO McLAREN HONDA	1'19.112	13	1'17.876■	5	204.371
2	2	A.PROST	FRA	MARLBORO McLAREN HONDA	1'20.401	9	1'18.773■	5	0.897
3	27	N.MANSELL	GBR	FERRARI	1'21.170	12	1'19.137■	6	1.261
4	16	I.CAPELLI	ITA	LEYTON HOUSE MARCH JUDD	1'24.720	6	1'19.337■	7	1.461
5	6	R.PATRESE	ITA	CANON WILLIAMS RENAULT	1'21.763	14	1'19.656■	7	1.780
6	28	G.BERGER	AUT	FERRARI	1'21.564	5	1'19.835■	5	1.959
7	4	M.ALBORETO	ITA	TYRRELL FORD	1'22.150	4	1'20.066■	15	2.190
8	5	T.BOUTSEN	BEL	CANON WILLIAMS RENAULT	1'21.456	9	1'20.234■	2	2.358
9	8	S.MODENA	ITA	BRABHAM JUDD	1'22.640	2	1'20.505■	10	2.629
10	9	D.WARWICK	GBR	USF&G ARROWS FORD	1'23.245	11	1'20.601■	3	2.725
11	26	O.GROUILLARD	FRA	LIGIER FORD	1'23.053	7	1'20.859■	4	2.983
12	22	A.DE CESARIS	ITA	BMS DALLARA FORD	1'23.066	6	1'20.873■	9	2.997
13	19	A.NANNINI	ITA	BENETTON FORD	1'21.791	16	1'20.888■	15	3.012
14	3	J.PALMER	GBR	TYRRELL FORD	1'21.561	11	1'20.888■	12	3.012
15	12	S.NAKAJIMA	JPN	CAMEL LOTUS JUDD	1'22.438	10	1'20.943■	5	3.067
16	30	P.ALLIOT	FRA	L.& C. LOLA LAMBORGHINI	1'22.014	3	1'21.031■	8	3.155
17	40	G.TARQUINI	ITA	AGS FORD	1'23.004	8	1'21.031■	13	3.155
18	20	J.HERBERT	GBR	BENETTON FORD	1'22.553	15	1'21.105■	11	3.229
19	21	A.CAFFI	ITA	BMS DALLARA FORD	1'22.705	4	1'21.139■	7	3.263
20	7	M.BRUNDLE	GBR	BRABHAM JUDD	1'23.375	5	1'21.217■	8	3.341
21	36	S.JOHANSSON	SWE	ONYX FORD	1'23.746	14	1'21.358■	2	3.482
22	23	P.MARTINI	ITA	SCM MINARDI FORD	1'24.181	17	1'21.471■	10	3.595
23	38	C.DANNER	BRD	RIAL FORD	1'22.931	9	1'21.696■	10	3.820
24	10	E.CHEEVER	USA	USF&G ARROWS FORD	1'23.427	4	1'21.716■	15	3.840
25	25	R.ARNOUX	FRA	LIGIER FORD	1'24.890	5	1'21.830■	4	3.954
26	11	N.PIQUET	BRA	CAMEL LOTUS JUDD	1'23.090	15	1'21.831■	10	3.955
27	24	L.SALA	SPA	SCM MINARDI FORD	1'26.567	7	1'21.935■	9	4.059
28	15	M.GUGELMIN	BRA	LEYTON HOUSE MARCH JUDD	1'22.712	8	1'22.081■	6	4.205
29	29	Y.DALMAS	FRA	L.& C. LOLA LAMBORGHINI	1'25.651■	2	9'27.789	2	7.775
30	31	R.MORENO	BRA	COLONI FORD		0	3'34.095■	1	2'16.219

1989 - MOLSON GRAND PRIX OF CANADA - MONTREAL
OFFICIAL PRACTICE TIMES

POS	NR	DRIVER	NAT	CAR	1st SESSION B.TIME LAP	2nd SESSION B.TIME LAP	km/h DIFF
1	2	A.PROST	FRA	MARLBORO McLAREN HONDA	1'20.973■10	1'22.269 8	195.176
2	1	A.SENNA	BRA	MARLBORO McLAREN HONDA	1'21.049■21	1'21.269 12	0.076
3	6	R.PATRESE	ITA	CANON WILLIAMS RENAULT	1'21.783■ 9	1'23.738 5	0.810
4	28	G.BERGER	AUT	FERRARI	1'21.946■ 6	1'22.305 2	0.973
5	27	N.MANSELL	GBR	FERRARI	1'22.165■18	1'22.751 10	1.192
6	5	T.BOUTSEN	BEL	CANON WILLIAMS RENAULT	1'22.311■ 9	1'24.004 11	1.338
7	8	S.MODENA	ITA	BRABHAM JUDD	1'22.612■ 6	1'23.599 4	1.639
8	21	A.CAFFI	ITA	BMS DALLARA FORD	1'22.901■ 9	1'24.957 5	1.928
9	22	A.DE CESARIS	ITA	BMS DALLARA FORD	1'23.050■18	1'24.444 4	2.077
10	30	P.ALLIOT	FRA	L.& C. LOLA LAMBORGHINI	1'23.059■ 9	0	2.086
11	23	P.MARTINI	ITA	SCM MINARDI FORD	1'23.252■ 7	1'25.195 3	2.279
12	9	D.WARWICK	GBR	USF&G ARROWS FORD	1'23.348■11	1'23.833 7	2.375
13	19	A.NANNINI	ITA	BENETTON FORD	1'23.542■21	1'24.279 6	2.569
14	3	J.PALMER	GBR	TYRRELL FORD	1'23.665■13	1'23.876 11	2.692
15	17	N.LARINI	ITA	OSELLA FORD	1'23.799■ 7	1'25.289 3	2.826
16	10	E.CHEEVER	USA	USF&G ARROWS FORD	1'23.828■19	1'24.693 6	2.855
17	15	M.GUGELMIN	BRA	LEYTON HOUSE MARCH JUDD	1'23.863■ 8	1'24.734 3	2.890
18	36	S.JOHANSSON	SWE	ONYX FORD	1'23.979■ 8	1'24.918 5	3.006
19	11	N.PIQUET	BRA	CAMEL LOTUS JUDD	1'24.029■ 4	1'25.825 8	3.056
20	4	M.ALBORETO	ITA	TYRRELL FORD	1'24.296■ 9	1'25.412 5	3.323
21	16	I.CAPELLI	ITA	LEYTON HOUSE MARCH JUDD	1'24.406■ 8	1'25.094 3	3.433
22	25	R.ARNOUX	FRA	LIGIER FORD	1'24.558■ 6	1'25.394 20	3.585
23	38	C.DANNER	BRD	RIAL FORD	1'25.298 7	1'24.727■11	3.754
24	24	L.SALA	SPA	SCM MINARDI FORD	1'24.786■12	1'25.570 5	3.813
25	40	G.TARQUINI	ITA	AGS FORD	1'24.793■ 9	1'25.246 6	3.820
26	31	R.MORENO	BRA	COLONI FORD	47'24.470 1	1'25.037■ 9	4.064
27	12	S.NAKAJIMA	JPN	CAMEL LOTUS JUDD	1'25.051■11	1'26.358 13	4.078
28	29	Y.DALMAS	FRA	L.& C. LOLA LAMBORGHINI	1'25.317 20	1'25.161■11	4.188
29	20	J.HERBERT	GBR	BENETTON FORD	1'25.335 14	1'25.282■ 6	4.309
30	26	O.GROUILLARD	FRA	LIGIER FORD	1'25.382 8	1'25.289■ 6	4.316

1989 - ICEBERG USA GRAND PRIX - PHOENIX
OFFICIAL PRACTICE TIMES

POS	NR	DRIVER	NAT	CAR	1st SESSION B.TIME LAP	2nd SESSION B.TIME LAP	mph DIFF
1	1	A.SENNA	BRA	MARLBORO McLAREN HONDA	1'30.108■16	1'30.710 9	94.287
2	2	A.PROST	FRA	MARLBORO McLAREN HONDA	1'31.620 5	1'31.517■ 7	1.409
3	19	A.NANNINI	ITA	BENETTON FORD	1'32.924 16	1'31.799■ 4	1.691
4	27	N.MANSELL	GBR	FERRARI	1'31.927■10	1'33.383 7	1.819
5	7	M.BRUNDLE	GBR	BRABHAM JUDD	1'32.750 3	1'31.960■ 9	1.852
6	21	A.CAFFI	ITA	BMS DALLARA FORD	1'32.819 10	1'32.160■ 6	2.052
7	8	S.MODENA	ITA	BRABHAM JUDD	1'34.267 12	1'32.286■ 3	2.178
8	28	G.BERGER	AUT	FERRARI	1'33.697 17	1'32.364■10	2.256
9	4	M.ALBORETO	ITA	TYRRELL FORD	1'33.377 17	1'32.491■ 5	2.383
10	9	D.WARWICK	GBR	USF&G ARROWS FORD	1'32.640 6	1'32.492■ 5	2.384
11	16	I.CAPELLI	ITA	LEYTON HOUSE MARCH JUDD	1'36.136 21	1'32.493■ 6	2.385
12	30	P.ALLIOT	FRA	L.& C. LOLA LAMBORGHINI	1'34.721 3	1'32.562■12	2.454
13	22	A.DE CESARIS	ITA	BMS DALLARA FORD	1'33.061 15	1'32.649■ 7	2.541
14	6	R.PATRESE	ITA	CANON WILLIAMS RENAULT	1'34.523 12	1'32.795■ 3	2.687
15	23	P.MARTINI	ITA	SCM MINARDI FORD	1'34.794 14	1'33.031■ 5	2.923
16	5	T.BOUTSEN	BEL	CANON WILLIAMS RENAULT	1'35.227 9	1'33.044■ 3	2.936
17	10	E.CHEEVER	USA	USF&G ARROWS FORD	1'33.214■ 6	1'33.361 10	3.106
18	15	M.GUGELMIN	BRA	LEYTON HOUSE MARCH JUDD	1'35.236 10	1'33.324■ 2	3.216
19	36	S.JOHANSSON	SWE	ONYX FORD	1'34.637 17	1'33.370■ 5	3.262
20	24	L.SALA	SPA	SCM MINARDI FORD	1'34.636 7	1'33.724■ 3	3.616
21	3	J.PALMER	GBR	TYRRELL FORD	1'34.748 12	1'33.741■15	3.633
22	11	N.PIQUET	BRA	CAMEL LOTUS JUDD	1'33.745■20	1'33.804 4	3.637
23	12	S.NAKAJIMA	JPN	CAMEL LOTUS JUDD	1'35.188 9	1'33.782■ 6	3.674
24	40	G.TARQUINI	ITA	AGS FORD	1'34.455 14	1'33.790■ 2	3.682
25	20	J.HERBERT	GBR	BENETTON FORD	1'35.377 15	1'33.806■ 4	3.698
26	38	C.DANNER	BRD	RIAL FORD	1'35.453 18	1'33.848■ 8	3.740
27	26	O.GROUILLARD	FRA	LIGIER FORD	1'35.124 9	1'34.153■11	4.045
28	31	R.MORENO	BRA	COLONI FORD	2'10.795 2	1'34.352■ 3	4.244
29	25	R.ARNOUX	FRA	LIGIER FORD	1'35.823 4	1'34.798■ 5	4.690
30	29	Y.DALMAS	FRA	L.& C. LOLA LAMBORGHINI	1'35.771 5	1'35.496■ 4	5.388

olivetti

1989 - FRENCH GRAND PRIX - LE CASTELLET
OFFICIAL PRACTICE TIMES

POS	NR	DRIVER	NAT	CAR	1st SESSION B.TIME LAP	2nd SESSION B.TIME LAP	km/h DIFF
1	2	A.PROST	FRA	MARLBORO McLAREN HONDA	1'08.285 5	1'07.203■ 4	204.259
2	1	A.SENNA	BRA	MARLBORO McLAREN HONDA	1'07.920 2	1'07.228■ 5	0.025
3	27	N.MANSELL	GBR	FERRARI	1'09.030 6	1'07.455■ 5	0.252
4	19	A.NANNINI	ITA	BENETTON FORD	1'09.615 7	1'08.137■ 8	0.934
5	5	T.BOUTSEN	BEL	CANON WILLIAMS RENAULT	1'08.299 7	1'08.211■ 6	1.008
6	28	G.BERGER	AUT	FERRARI	1'09.011 3	1'08.233■ 2	1.030
7	30	P.ALLIOT	FRA	LOLA LAMBORGHINI	1'09.478 2	1'08.561■ 2	1.358
8	6	R.PATRESE	ITA	CANON WILLIAMS RENAULT	1'09.326 3	1'08.993■ 8	1.790
9	3	J.PALMER	GBR	TYRRELL FORD	1'10.238 5	1'09.026■ 4	1.823
10	15	M.GUGELMIN	BRA	LEYTON HOUSE MARCH JUDD	1'10.122 2	1'09.036■ 5	1.833
11	37	B.GACHOT	BEL	ONYX FORD	1'10.564 2	1'09.122■ 7	1.919
12	16	I.CAPELLI	ITA	LEYTON HOUSE MARCH JUDD	1'09.569 3	1'09.283■ 4	2.080
13	36	S.JOHANSSON	SWE	ONYX FORD	1'10.600 6	1'09.299■ 7	2.096
14	9	M.DONNELLY	IRL	USF&G ARROWS FORD	1'11.223 4	1'09.524■ 5	2.321
15	29	E.BERNARD	FRA	LOLA LAMBORGHINI	1'25.401 2	1'09.596■ 7	2.393
16	4	J.ALESI	FRA	TYRRELL FORD	1'09.668■ 6	1'09.909 4	2.465
17	26	O.GROUILLARD	FRA	LIGIER FORD	1'10.410 8	1'09.717■ 2	2.514
18	25	R.ARNOUX	FRA	LIGIER FORD	1'10.725 2	1'10.077■ 2	2.874
19	12	S.NAKAJIMA	JPN	CAMEL LOTUS JUDD	1'12.125 5	1'10.119■ 7	2.916
20	11	N.PIQUET	BRA	CAMEL LOTUS JUDD	1'10.473 2	1'10.135■ 5	2.932
21	40	G.TARQUINI	ITA	AGS FORD	1'11.136 2	1'10.216■ 6	3.013
22	8	S.MODENA	ITA	BRABHAM JUDD	1'10.910 2	1'10.254■ 2	3.051
23	23	P.MARTINI	ITA	SCM MINARDI FORD	1'10.640 8	1'10.267■ 8	3.064
24	20	E.PIRRO	ITA	BENETTON FORD	1'11.566 4	1'10.292■ 2	3.089
25	10	E.CHEEVER	USA	USF&G ARROWS FORD	1'10.372■ 5	0	3.169
26	21	A.CAFFI	ITA	BMS DALLARA FORD	1'11.409 7	1'10.468■ 6	3.265
27	22	A.DE CESARIS	ITA	BMS DALLARA FORD	1'12.078 7	1'10.591■ 4	3.388
28	24	L.SALA	SPA	SCM MINARDI FORD	1'11.539 8	1'11.079■ 2	3.876
29	38	C.DANNER	BRD	RIAL FORD	1'12.569 10	1'11.178■10	3.975
30	31	R.MORENO	BRA	COLONI FORD	1'14.746 3	1'11.372■ 5	4.169

1989 - SHELL BRITISH GRAND PRIX - SILVERSTONE
OFFICIAL PRACTICE TIMES

POS	NR	DRIVER	NAT	CAR	1st SESSION B.TIME LAP	2nd SESSION B.TIME LAP	mph DIFF
1	1	A.SENNA	BRA	MARLBORO McLAREN HONDA	1'09.124 2	1'09.099■ 9	154.735
2	2	A.PROST	FRA	MARLBORO McLAREN HONDA	1'10.156 4	1'09.266■ 4	0.167
3	27	N.MANSELL	GBR	FERRARI	1'09.488■ 5	1'10.279 2	0.389
4	28	G.BERGER	AUT	FERRARI	1'09.855■ 4	1'10.130 4	0.756
5	6	R.PATRESE	ITA	WILLIAMS RENAULT	1'09.865■ 4	1'09.963 4	0.766
6	15	M.GUGELMIN	BRA	LEYTON HOUSE MARCH JUDD	1'10.336■ 5	1'12.665 5	1.237
7	5	T.BOUTSEN	BEL	WILLIAMS RENAULT	1'10.376■ 4	1'10.771 2	1.277
8	16	I.CAPELLI	ITA	LEYTON HOUSE MARCH JUDD	1'10.650■ 7	1'11.544 2	1.551
9	19	A.NANNINI	ITA	BENETTON FORD	1'11.034 6	1'10.798■ 6	1.699
10	11	N.PIQUET	BRA	CAMEL LOTUS JUDD	1'11.589 6	1'10.925■ 6	1.826
11	23	P.MARTINI	ITA	SCM MINARDI FORD	1'11.368■ 9	1'11.582 4	2.269
12	30	P.ALLIOT	FRA	L.& C. LOLA LAMBORGHINI	1'11.541■ 8	1'12.408 4	2.442
13	29	E.BERNARD	FRA	L.& C. LOLA LAMBORGHINI	1'12.193 10	1'11.687■ 4	2.588
14	8	S.MODENA	ITA	BRABHAM JUDD	1'12.262 11	1'11.755■ 3	2.656
15	24	L.SALA	SPA	SCM MINARDI FORD	1'11.955 9	1'11.826■ 6	2.727
16	12	S.NAKAJIMA	JPN	CAMEL LOTUS JUDD	1'12.326 9	1'11.960■ 8	2.861
17	17	N.LARINI	ITA	OSELLA FORD	1'12.061■ 6	1'12.395 9	2.962
18	3	J.PALMER	GBR	TYRRELL FORD	1'12.070■20	1'12.157 4	2.971
19	9	D.WARWICK	GBR	USF&G ARROWS FORD	1'12.295 5	1'12.208■ 7	3.109
20	7	M.BRUNDLE	GBR	BRABHAM JUDD	1'12.616 11	1'12.327■ 8	3.228
21	37	B.GACHOT	BEL	ONYX FORD	1'12.329■ 7	1'12.928 7	3.230
22	4	J.ALESI	FRA	TYRRELL FORD	1'12.994 15	1'12.341■ 5	3.242
23	31	R.MORENO	BRA	COLONI FORD	1'12.680 11	1'12.412■13	3.313
24	26	O.GROUILLARD	FRA	LIGIER FORD	1'12.853 19	1'12.605■ 6	3.506
25	22	A.DE CESARIS	ITA	BMS DALLARA FORD	1'13.335 12	1'12.904■ 9	3.805
26	20	E.PIRRO	ITA	BENETTON FORD	1'13.233 2	1'13.148■ 4	4.049
27	25	R.ARNOUX	FRA	LIGIER FORD	1'13.240■ 4	1'13.550 8	4.141
28	10	E.CHEEVER	USA	USF&G ARROWS FORD	1'13.655 2	1'13.386■12	4.287
29	40	G.TARQUINI	ITA	AGS FORD	1'13.496■ 5	1'13.997 2	4.397
30	38	C.DANNER	BRD	RIAL FORD	1'15.387■14	1'15.394 4	6.288

1989 - GERMAN GRAND PRIX - HOCKENHEIMRING
OFFICIAL PRACTICE TIMES

POS	NR	DRIVER	NAT	CAR	1st SESSION B.TIME LAP	2nd SESSION B.TIME LAP	km/h DIFF
1	1	A.SENNA	BRA	MARLBORO McLAREN HONDA	1'42.300■ 4	1'42.790 2	239.191
2	2	A.PROST	FRA	MARLBORO McLAREN HONDA	1'43.306 4	1'43.295■ 6	0.995
3	27	N.MANSELL	GBR	FERRARI	1'44.020■ 4	1'44.076 4	1.720
4	28	G.BERGER	AUT	FERRARI	1'44.467 2	1'44.509 4	2.167
5	6	R.PATRESE	ITA	WILLIAMS RENAULT	1'45.062 4	1'44.511■ 2	2.211
6	5	T.BOUTSEN	BEL	WILLIAMS RENAULT	1'45.520 5	1'44.702■ 2	2.402
7	19	A.NANNINI	ITA	BENETTON FORD	1'45.033■ 8	1'45.040 5	2.733
8	11	N.PIQUET	BRA	CAMEL LOTUS JUDD	1'47.316 5	1'45.475■ 6	3.175
9	20	E.PIRRO	ITA	BENETTON FORD	1'46.521 6	1'45.845■ 6	3.545
10	4	J.ALESI	FRA	TYRRELL FORD	1'47.551 4	1'46.888■ 5	4.588
11	26	O.GROUILLARD	FRA	LIGIER FORD	1'47.408 2	1'46.893■ 6	4.593
12	7	M.BRUNDLE	GBR	BRABHAM JUDD	1'47.216■ 2	1'47.796 4	4.916
13	23	P.MARTINI	ITA	SCM MINARDI FORD	1'48.222 2	1'47.380■ 6	5.080
14	15	M.GUGELMIN	BRA	LEYTON HOUSE MARCH JUDD	1'47.387■ 4	1'47.578 2	5.087
15	30	P.ALLIOT	FRA	LOLA LAMBORGHINI	1'47.486■ 4	1'47.566 2	5.186
16	8	S.MODENA	ITA	BRABHAM JUDD	1'47.511■ 7	1'47.552 5	5.211
17	9	D.WARWICK	GBR	USF&G ARROWS FORD	1'47.756 2	1'47.533■ 3	5.233
18	12	S.NAKAJIMA	JPN	CAMEL LOTUS JUDD	1'48.782 2	1'47.663■ 2	5.363
19	3	J.PALMER	GBR	TYRRELL FORD	1'47.836 2	1'47.676■ 2	5.376
20	21	A.CAFFI	ITA	BMS DALLARA FORD	1'48.671 6	1'47.679■ 2	5.379
21	22	A.DE CESARIS	ITA	BMS DALLARA FORD	1'47.879■ 4	1'48.005 6	5.579
22	16	I.CAPELLI	ITA	LEYTON HOUSE MARCH JUDD	1'48.239 4	1'48.078■ 4	5.778
23	25	R.ARNOUX	FRA	LIGIER FORD	1'48.266 2	1'48.598 4	5.966
24	36	S.JOHANSSON	SWE	ONYX FORD	1'49.935 3	1'48.348■ 6	6.048
25	10	E.CHEEVER	USA	USF&G ARROWS FORD	1'48.396 6	1'48.553 2	6.096
26	29	M.ALBORETO	ITA	LOLA LAMBORGHINI	1'48.670 5	1'48.726 2	6.370
27	24	L.SALA	SPA	SCM MINARDI FORD	1'49.587 9	1'48.686■ 7	6.386
28	37	B.GACHOT	BEL	ONYX FORD	1'49.252 6	1'49.004■ 7	6.704
29	38	C.DANNER	FRG	RIAL FORD	1'50.679 7	1'49.767■ 2	7.467
30	39	V.WEIDLER	FRG	RIAL FORD	1'50.673 2	1'49.770■ 9	7.470

1989 - POP 84 HUNGARIAN GRAND PRIX - BUDAPEST
OFFICIAL PRACTICE TIMES

POS	NR	DRIVER	NAT	CAR	1st SESSION B.TIME LAP	2nd SESSION B.TIME LAP	km/h DIFF
1	6	R.PATRESE	ITA	WILLIAMS RENAULT	1'19.726■ 4	1'20.644 2	179.174
2	1	A.SENNA	BRA	MARLBORO McLAREN HONDA	1'21.576 2	1'20.039■ 4	0.313
3	21	A.CAFFI	ITA	BMS DALLARA FORD	1'21.040 4	1'20.704■ 6	0.978
4	5	T.BOUTSEN	BEL	WILLIAMS RENAULT	1'23.492 8	1'21.001■ 2	1.275
5	2	A.PROST	FRA	MARLBORO McLAREN HONDA	1'21.076■ 2	1'22.267 2	1.350
6	28	G.BERGER	AUT	FERRARI	1'21.304 2	1'21.270■ 2	1.544
7	19	A.NANNINI	ITA	BENETTON FORD	1'21.448 13	1'21.301■ 3	1.575
8	8	S.MODENA	ITA	BRABHAM JUDD	1'23.090 4	1'21.472■11	1.746
9	9	D.WARWICK	GBR	USF&G ARROWS FORD	1'23.111 6	1'21.617■ 4	1.891
10	23	P.MARTINI	ITA	SCM MINARDI FORD	1'21.746■ 5	1'32.546 2	2.020
11	4	J.ALESI	FRA	TYRRELL FORD	1'23.853 5	1'21.799■ 4	2.073
12	27	N.MANSELL	GBR	FERRARI	1'22.544 3	1'21.951■13	2.225
13	15	M.GUGELMIN	BRA	LEYTON HOUSE MARCH JUDD	1'22.949 4	1'22.083■ 4	2.357
14	16	I.CAPELLI	ITA	LEYTON HOUSE MARCH JUDD	1'22.445 6	1'22.088■ 6	2.362
15	7	M.BRUNDLE	GBR	BRABHAM JUDD	1'22.970 4	1'22.296■ 2	2.570
16	10	E.CHEEVER	USA	USF&G ARROWS FORD	1'23.251 4	1'22.374■ 5	2.648
17	11	N.PIQUET	BRA	CAMEL LOTUS JUDD	1'22.837 2	1'22.406■ 6	2.680
18	22	A.DE CESARIS	ITA	BMS DALLARA FORD	1'23.463 9	1'22.410■ 2	2.684
19	3	J.PALMER	GBR	TYRRELL FORD	1'24.670 3	1'22.578■ 4	2.852
20	12	S.NAKAJIMA	JPN	CAMEL LOTUS JUDD	1'23.996 7	1'22.630■ 6	2.904
21	37	B.GACHOT	BEL	ONYX FORD	1'22.634■ 6	1'23.720 2	2.908
22	18	P.GHINZANI	ITA	OSELLA FORD	1'23.091 6	1'22.763■ 4	3.037
23	24	L.SALA	SPA	SCM MINARDI FORD	1'23.017■ 5	1'24.188 5	3.291
24	36	S.JOHANSSON	SWE	ONYX FORD	1'23.372 4	1'23.148■ 2	3.422
25	20	E.PIRRO	ITA	BENETTON FORD	1'23.772 11	1'23.399■ 2	3.673
26	29	M.ALBORETO	ITA	LOLA LAMBORGHINI	1'23.733■ 8	1'25.660 4	4.007
27	25	R.ARNOUX	FRA	LIGIER FORD	1'25.862 6	1'24.003■11	4.277
28	26	O.GROUILLARD	FRA	LIGIER FORD	1'24.702■ 6	1'25.169 4	4.976
29	38	C.DANNER	FRG	RIAL FORD	1'26.485 2	1'25.017■ 6	5.291
30	39	V.WEIDLER	FRG	RIAL FORD	0	1'26.320■ 3	6.594

1989 - BELGIAN GRAND PRIX - SPA
OFFICIAL PRACTICE TIMES

POS	NR	DRIVER	NAT	CAR	1st SESSION B.TIME LAP	2nd SESSION B.TIME LAP	km/h DIFF
1	1	A.SENNA	BRA	MARLBORO McLAREN HONDA	2'11.171 6	1'50.867■ 4	225.351
2	2	A.PROST	FRA	MARLBORO McLAREN HONDA	2'12.721 5	1'51.463■ 4	0.596
3	28	G.BERGER	AUT	FERRARI	2'11.102 7	1'52.391■ 4	1.524
4	5	T.BOUTSEN	BEL	WILLIAMS RENAULT	2'13.030 15	1'52.786■ 2	1.919
5	6	R.PATRESE	ITA	WILLIAMS RENAULT	2'12.581 17	1'52.875■ 4	2.008
6	27	N.MANSELL	GBR	FERRARI	2'12.042 6	1'52.898■ 4	2.031
7	19	A.NANNINI	ITA	BENETTON FORD	2'14.117 11	1'55.075■ 8	4.208
8	8	S.MODENA	ITA	BRABHAM JUDD	2'19.161 10	1'55.642■ 7	4.775
9	15	M.GUGELMIN	BRA	LEYTON HOUSE MARCH JUDD	2'16.401 13	1'55.729■ 7	4.862
10	9	D.WARWICK	GBR	USF&G ARROWS FORD	2'13.005 14	1'55.864■ 5	4.997
11	30	P.ALLIOT	FRA	LOLA LAMBORGHINI	2'14.357 4	1'55.890■ 4	5.023
12	21	A.CAFFI	ITA	BMS DALLARA FORD	2'17.604 17	1'55.892■ 4	5.025
13	20	E.PIRRO	ITA	BENETTON FORD	2'15.068 7	1'55.902■11	5.035
14	23	P.MARTINI	ITA	SCM MINARDI FORD	2'15.515 13	1'56.115■ 7	5.248
15	36	S.JOHANSSON	SWE	ONYX FORD	2'17.329 14	1'56.129■ 8	5.262
16	4	J.HERBERT	GBR	TYRRELL FORD	2'17.714 10	1'56.248■ 5	5.381
17	25	R.ARNOUX	FRA	LIGIER FORD	2'14.344 16	1'56.251■ 5	5.384
18	22	A.DE CESARIS	ITA	BMS DALLARA FORD	2'17.512 10	1'56.257■10	5.390
19	16	I.CAPELLI	ITA	LEYTON HOUSE MARCH JUDD	2'15.863 12	1'56.291■ 7	5.424
20	7	M.BRUNDLE	GBR	BRABHAM JUDD	2'18.663 10	1'56.327■ 7	5.460
21	3	J.PALMER	GBR	TYRRELL FORD	2'18.405 4	1'56.600■ 5	5.733
22	29	M.ALBORETO	ITA	LOLA LAMBORGHINI	2'17.240 2	1'56.616■ 7	5.749
23	37	B.GACHOT	BEL	ONYX FORD	2'18.151 12	1'56.716■ 6	5.849
24	10	E.CHEEVER	USA	USF&G ARROWS FORD	2'14.641 16	1'56.748■ 4	5.881
25	24	L.SALA	SPA	SCM MINARDI FORD	2'18.907 14	1'56.957■10	6.090
26	26	O.GROUILLARD	FRA	LIGIER FORD	2'18.175 12	1'57.027■ 7	6.160
27	12	S.NAKAJIMA	JPN	CAMEL LOTUS JUDD	2'13.677 20	1'57.251■ 5	6.384
28	11	N.PIQUET	BRA	CAMEL LOTUS JUDD	2'14.358 14	1'57.771■ 4	6.904
29	38	C.DANNER	FRG	RIAL FORD	2'20.503 4	2'00.247■ 2	9.380
30	39	P.RAPHANEL	FRA	RIAL FORD	2'21.180 6	2'02.937■ 7	12.070

1989 - COCA COLA ITALIAN GRAND PRIX - MONZA
OFFICIAL PRACTICE TIMES

POS	NR	DRIVER	NAT	CAR	1st SESSION B.TIME LAP	2nd SESSION B.TIME LAP	km/h DIFF
1	1	A.SENNA	BRA	MARLBORO McLAREN HONDA	1'25.021 15	1'23.720■ 4	249.403
2	28	G.BERGER	AUT	FERRARI	1'24.734■ 5	1'24.998 8	1.014
3	27	N.MANSELL	GBR	FERRARI	1'24.739■ 8	1'24.979 7	1.019
4	2	A.PROST	FRA	MARLBORO McLAREN HONDA	1'25.872 2	1'25.510■ 8	1.790
5	6	R.PATRESE	ITA	WILLIAMS RENAULT	1'26.195 4	1'25.545■ 4	1.825
6	5	T.BOUTSEN	BEL	WILLIAMS RENAULT	1'26.155■ 4	1'26.392 4	2.435
7	30	P.ALLIOT	FRA	LOLA LAMBORGHINI	1'27.118 6	1'26.985■ 2	3.265
8	19	A.NANNINI	ITA	BENETTON FORD	1'27.162 5	1'27.052■17	3.332
9	20	E.PIRRO	ITA	BENETTON FORD	1'28.367 7	1'27.397■10	3.677
10	4	J.ALESI	FRA	TYRRELL FORD	0	1'27.399■ 6	3.679
11	11	N.PIQUET	BRA	CAMEL LOTUS JUDD	1'28.135 8	1'27.508■ 7	3.788
12	7	M.BRUNDLE	GBR	BRABHAM JUDD	1'27.627■ 5	1'27.637 5	3.907
13	29	M.ALBORETO	ITA	LOLA LAMBORGHINI	1'28.586 9	1'27.803■ 5	4.083
14	3	J.PALMER	GBR	TYRRELL FORD	1'29.187 6	1'27.822■10	4.102
15	23	P.MARTINI	ITA	SCM MINARDI FORD	1'28.397 6	1'27.923■ 6	4.203
16	9	D.WARWICK	GBR	USF&G ARROWS FORD	1'28.092 6	1'29.031 2	4.372
17	22	A.DE CESARIS	ITA	BMS DALLARA FORD	1'28.129■ 8	1'28.180 11	4.409
18	16	I.CAPELLI	ITA	LEYTON HOUSE MARCH JUDD	1'31.969 2	1'28.430■ 9	4.710
19	12	S.NAKAJIMA	JPN	CAMEL LOTUS JUDD	1'28.769 14	1'28.441■25	4.721
20	21	A.CAFFI	ITA	BMS DALLARA FORD	1'28.596■ 5	1'28.708 9	4.876
21	26	O.GROUILLARD	FRA	LIGIER FORD	1'28.669■ 7	1'29.537 12	4.949
22	37	B.GACHOT	BEL	ONYX FORD	1'28.684■ 4	1'29.058 5	4.964
23	25	R.ARNOUX	FRA	LIGIER FORD	1'28.685■ 4	1'28.843 5	4.965
24	17	N.LARINI	ITA	OSELLA FORD	1'29.265 10	1'28.773■ 3	5.053
25	15	M.GUGELMIN	BRA	LEYTON HOUSE MARCH JUDD	1'29.192 6	1'28.923■ 3	5.203
26	24	L.SALA	SPA	SCM MINARDI FORD	1'29.592 9	1'29.293■11	5.573
27	10	E.CHEEVER	USA	USF&G ARROWS FORD	1'29.884 14	1'29.554■ 6	5.834
28	38	C.DANNER	FRG	RIAL FORD	1'32.074 12	1'31.830■ 8	8.110
29	39	P.RAPHANEL	FRA	RIAL FORD	0	1'36.295■ 3	12.575

olivetti

1989 - PORTUGUESE GRAND PRIX - ESTORIL
OFFICIAL PRACTICE TIMES

POS	NR	DRIVER	NAT	CAR	1st SESSION B.TIME LAP	2nd SESSION B.TIME LAP	km/h DIFF
1	1	A.SENNA	BRA	MARLBORO McLAREN HONDA	1'15.496 4	1'15.468■ 3	207.505
2	28	G.BERGER	AUT	FERRARI	1'16.799 4	1'16.059■ 5	0.591
3	27	N.MANSELL	GBR	FERRARI	1'17.387 4	1'16.193■ 2	0.725
4	2	A.PROST	FRA	MARLBORO McLAREN HONDA	1'17.336 4	1'16.204■ 6	0.736
5	23	P.MARTINI	ITA	SCM MINARDI FORD	1'16.938■ 6	1'17.161 4	1.470
6	6	R.PATRESE	ITA	WILLIAMS RENAULT	1'17.281■ 4	1'17.852 15	1.813
7	21	A.CAFFI	ITA	BMS DALLARA FORD	1'18.623 5	1'17.661■ 4	2.193
8	5	T.BOUTSEN	BEL	WILLIAMS RENAULT	1'17.801■ 4	1'17.888 10	2.333
9	24	L.SALA	SPA	SCM MINARDI FORD	1'17.844■ 7	1'18.305 5	2.376
10	7	M.BRUNDLE	GBR	BRABHAM JUDD	1'17.874■ 2	1'17.995 4	2.406
11	8	S.MODENA	ITA	BRABHAM JUDD	1'18.589 2	1'18.093■ 8	2.625
12	36	S.JOHANSSON	SWE	ONYX FORD	1'19.281 2	1'18.105■ 2	2.637
13	19	A.NANNINI	ITA	BENETTON FORD	1'18.115■11	1'18.359 12	2.647
14	15	M.GUGELMIN	BRA	LEYTON HOUSE MARCH JUDD	1'18.124■ 6	1'18.277 8	2.656
15	31	R.MORENO	BRA	COLONI FORD	1'18.196■ 8	1'20.512 3	2.728
16	20	E.PIRRO	ITA	BENETTON FORD	1'18.340 9	1'18.328■ 7	2.860
17	30	P.ALLIOT	FRA	LOLA LAMBORGHINI	1'19.306 4	1'18.386■ 6	2.918
18	3	J.PALMER	GBR	TYRRELL FORD	1'19.172 2	1'18.404■ 3	2.936
19	22	A.DE CESARIS	ITA	BMS DALLARA FORD	1'18.442■11	1'18.511 3	2.974
20	11	N.PIQUET	BRA	CAMEL LOTUS JUDD	1'18.482■10	1'18.682 4	3.014
21	29	M.ALBORETO	ITA	LOLA LAMBORGHINI	1'18.563■ 7	1'18.846 6	3.095
22	9	D.WARWICK	GBR	USF&G ARROWS FORD	1'18.711■ 4	1'18.892 3	3.243
23	25	R.ARNOUX	FRA	LIGIER FORD	1'18.767■ 2	1'19.979 6	3.299
24	16	I.CAPELLI	ITA	LEYTON HOUSE MARCH JUDD	1'19.079 4	1'18.785■ 2	3.317
25	12	S.NAKAJIMA	JPN	CAMEL LOTUS JUDD	1'19.278 9	1'19.165■ 5	3.697
26	10	E.CHEEVER	USA	USF&G ARROWS FORD	1'19.247■17	1'20.006 2	3.779
27	4	J.HERBERT	GBR	TYRRELL FORD	1'19.515 6	1'19.264■ 2	3.796
28	26	O.GROUILLARD	FRA	LIGIER FORD	1'19.605 7	1'19.436■ 6	3.968
29	39	P.RAPHANEL	FRA	RIAL FORD	0	1'21.435■ 4	5.967
30	38	C.DANNER	FRG	RIAL FORD	1'21.678■ 2	1'22.423 4	6.210

1989 - TIO PEPE SPANISH GRAND PRIX - JEREZ
OFFICIAL PRACTICE TIMES

POS	NR	DRIVER	NAT	CAR	1st SESSION B.TIME LAP	2nd SESSION B.TIME LAP	km/h DIFF
1	1	A.SENNA	BRA	MARLBORO McLAREN HONDA	1'21.855 7	1'20.291■ 4	189.122
2	28	G.BERGER	AUT	FERRARI	1'22.276 4	1'20.565■ 5	0.274
3	2	A.PROST	FRA	MARLBORO McLAREN HONDA	1'23.113 6	1'21.368■ 4	1.077
4	23	P.MARTINI	ITA	SCM MINARDI FORD	1'22.243 6	1'21.479■ 6	1.188
5	30	P.ALLIOT	FRA	LOLA LAMBORGHINI	1'23.597 5	1'21.708■ 2	1.417
6	6	R.PATRESE	ITA	WILLIAMS RENAULT	1'24.033 13	1'21.777■ 5	1.486
7	11	N.PIQUET	BRA	CAMEL LOTUS JUDD	1'23.235 9	1'21.922■ 4	1.631
8	7	M.BRUNDLE	GBR	BRABHAM JUDD	1'23.761 2	1'22.133■ 8	1.842
9	4	J.ALESI	FRA	TYRRELL FORD	1'24.615 4	1'22.363■ 4	2.072
10	20	E.PIRRO	ITA	BENETTON FORD	1'24.647 9	1'22.567■ 5	2.276
11	17	N.LARINI	ITA	OSELLA FORD	1'23.538 6	1'22.620■ 4	2.329
12	8	S.MODENA	ITA	BRABHAM JUDD	1'23.679 9	1'22.826■ 2	2.535
13	3	J.PALMER	GBR	TYRRELL FORD	1'23.494 4	1'23.052■ 2	2.761
14	19	A.NANNINI	ITA	BENETTON FORD	1'24.233 13	1'23.105■ 6	2.814
15	22	A.DE CESARIS	ITA	BMS DALLARA FORD	1'24.900 4	1'23.186■ 6	2.895
16	9	D.WARWICK	GBR	USF&G ARROWS FORD	1'24.161 4	1'23.222■ 4	2.931
17	37	J.LEHTO	FIN	ONYX FORD	1'24.322 4	1'23.243■ 2	2.952
18	12	S.NAKAJIMA	JPN	CAMEL LOTUS JUDD	0	1'23.309■ 7	3.018
19	16	I.CAPELLI	ITA	LEYTON HOUSE MARCH JUDD	1'23.401■ 5	0	3.110
20	24	L.SALA	SPA	SCM MINARDI FORD	1'23.908 6	1'23.443■ 7	3.152
21	5	T.BOUTSEN	BEL	WILLIAMS RENAULT	1'24.839 4	1'23.657■ 6	3.366
22	10	E.CHEEVER	USA	USF&G ARROWS FORD	1'24.222 4	1'23.729■ 2	3.438
23	21	A.CAFFI	ITA	BMS DALLARA FORD	1'24.658 6	1'23.763■ 6	3.472
24	26	O.GROUILLARD	FRA	LIGIER FORD	1'24.991 9	1'23.931■ 6	3.640
25	18	P.GHINZANI	ITA	OSELLA FORD	1'26.147 5	1'24.003■ 6	3.712
26	15	M.GUGELMIN	BRA	LEYTON HOUSE MARCH JUDD	1'24.707■ 7	0	4.416
27	25	R.ARNOUX	FRA	LIGIER FORD	1'26.767 2	1'25.190■ 2	4.899
28	39	P.RAPHANEL	FRA	RIAL FORD	1'28.311 2	1'25.443■ 5	5.152
29	38	G.FOITEK	SUI	RIAL FORD	1'29.226■ 4	0	8.935

olivetti

- FUJI TELEVISION JAPANESE GRAND PRIX - SUZUKA
OFFICIAL PRACTICE TIMES

POS	NR	DRIVER	NAT	CAR	1st SESSION B.TIME LAP	2nd SESSION B.TIME LAP	km/h DIFF
1	1	A.SENNA	BRA	MARLBORO McLAREN HONDA	1'39.493 10	1'38.041■ 5	215.139
2	2	A.PROST	FRA	MARLBORO McLAREN HONDA	1'40.875 5	1'39.771■ 4	1.730
3	28	G.BERGER	AUT	FERRARI	1'41.253 4	1'40.187■ 4	2.146
4	27	N.MANSELL	GBR	FERRARI	1'40.608 4	1'40.406■ 2	2.365
5	6	R.PATRESE	ITA	WILLIAMS RENAULT	1'42.397 10	1'40.936■ 6	2.895
6	19	A.NANNINI	ITA	BENETTON FORD	1'41.601 7	1'41.103■ 5	3.062
7	5	T.BOUTSEN	BEL	WILLIAMS RENAULT	1'42.943 10	1'41.324■ 4	3.283
8	30	P.ALLIOT	FRA	LOLA LAMBORGHINI	1'42.534 4	1'41.336■ 2	3.295
9	8	S.MODENA	ITA	BRABHAM JUDD	1'42.909 7	1'41.458■ 6	3.417
10	17	N.LARINI	ITA	OSELLA FORD	1'42.483 6	1'41.519■ 6	3.478
11	11	N.PIQUET	BRA	CAMEL LOTUS JUDD	1'43.386 7	1'41.802■ 4	3.761
12	12	S.NAKAJIMA	JPN	CAMEL LOTUS JUDD	1'43.370 11	1'41.988■11	3.947
13	7	M.BRUNDLE	GBR	BRABHAM JUDD	1'44.236 3	1'42.182■ 9	4.141
14	24	L.SALA	SPA	SCM MINARDI FORD	1'43.107 4	1'42.283■ 6	4.242
15	21	A.CAFFI	ITA	BMS DALLARA FORD	1'43.171 8	1'42.488■ 6	4.447
16	22	A.DE CESARIS	ITA	BMS DALLARA FORD	1'43.904 4	1'42.581■ 7	4.540
17	16	I.CAPELLI	ITA	LEYTON HOUSE MARCH JUDD	1'43.851 6	1'42.672■13	4.631
18	4	J.ALESI	FRA	TYRRELL FORD	1'43.306 4	1'42.709■ 2	4.668
19	23	P.BARILLA	ITA	SCM MINARDI FORD	1'46.096 9	1'42.780■ 4	4.739
20	15	M.GUGELMIN	BRA	LEYTON HOUSE MARCH JUDD	1'44.805 2	1'42.880■ 6	4.839
21	34	B.SCHNEIDER	FRG	WEST ZAKSPEED YAMAHA	1'44.323 2	1'42.892■ 2	4.851
22	20	E.PIRRO	ITA	BENETTON FORD	1'43.217 6	1'43.063■ 5	5.022
23	26	O.GROUILLARD	FRA	LIGIER FORD	1'45.801 12	1'43.379■ 4	5.338
24	10	E.CHEEVER	USA	USF&G ARROWS FORD	1'44.501 9	1'43.511■14	5.470
25	9	D.WARWICK	GBR	USF&G ARROWS FORD	1'44.288 4	1'43.599■ 2	5.558
26	3	J.PALMER	GBR	TYRRELL FORD	1'43.955 3	1'43.757■ 5	5.716
27	25	R.ARNOUX	FRA	LIGIER FORD	1'44.221 10	1'44.030■ 8	5.989
28	29	M.ALBORETO	ITA	LOLA LAMBORGHINI	1'44.063■ 4	1'44.101 8	6.022
29	38	P.RAPHANEL	FRA	RIAL FORD	2'11.328 2	1'47.160■ 4	9.119
30	39	B.GACHOT	BEL	RIAL FORD	1'50.883 6	1'47.295■ 6	9.254

1989 - FOSTER'S AUSTRALIAN GRAND PRIX - ADELAIDE
OFFICIAL PRACTICE TIMES

POS	NR	DRIVER	NAT	CAR	1st SESSION B.TIME LAP	2nd SESSION B.TIME LAP	km/h DIFF
1	1	A.SENNA	BRA	MARLBORO McLAREN HONDA	1'17.712 13	1'16.665■ 4	177.500
2	2	A.PROST	FRA	MARLBORO McLAREN HONDA	1'17.403■13	1'17.624 4	0.738
3	23	P.MARTINI	ITA	SCM MINARDI FORD	1'18.043 7	1'17.623■ 8	0.958
4	19	A.NANNINI	ITA	BENETTON FORD	1'18.271 10	1'17.762■ 6	1.097
5	5	T.BOUTSEN	BEL	WILLIAMS RENAULT	1'17.791■15	1'18.586 3	1.126
6	6	R.PATRESE	ITA	WILLIAMS RENAULT	1'18.636 18	1'17.827■ 3	1.162
7	27	N.MANSELL	GBR	FERRARI	1'19.525 15	1'18.313■ 5	1.648
8	8	S.MODENA	ITA	BRABHAM JUDD	1'18.750■ 9	1'20.076 3	2.085
9	22	A.DE CESARIS	ITA	BMS DALLARA FORD	1'18.828■ 6	1'19.487 10	2.163
10	21	A.CAFFI	ITA	BMS DALLARA FORD	1'18.857■ 4	1'18.899 6	2.192
11	17	N.LARINI	ITA	OSELLA FORD	1'19.305 8	1'19.110■ 6	2.445
12	7	M.BRUNDLE	GBR	BRABHAM JUDD	1'19.136■ 9	1'19.428 2	2.471
13	20	E.PIRRO	ITA	BENETTON FORD	1'19.710 7	1'19.217■ 5	2.552
14	28	G.BERGER	AUT	FERRARI	1'19.238■10	1'20.615 4	2.573
15	4	J.ALESI	FRA	TYRRELL FORD	1'19.363 2	1'19.259■ 9	2.594
16	16	I.CAPELLI	ITA	LEYTON HOUSE MARCH JUDD	1'19.269■ 3	1'19.294 5	2.604
17	37	J.LEHTO	FIN	ONYX FORD	1'20.767 11	1'19.309■ 5	2.644
18	11	N.PIQUET	BRA	CAMEL LOTUS JUDD	1'19.392■15	1'20.622 9	2.727
19	30	P.ALLIOT	FRA	LOLA LAMBORGHINI	1'19.568■12	1'19.579 3	2.903
20	9	D.WARWICK	GBR	USF&G ARROWS FORD	1'19.599■ 8	1'19.622 3	2.934
21	18	P.GHINZANI	ITA	OSELLA FORD	1'19.691■ 2	1'20.718 6	3.026
22	10	E.CHEEVER	USA	USF&G ARROWS FORD	1'19.922■11	1'21.206 3	3.257
23	12	S.NAKAJIMA	JPN	CAMEL LOTUS JUDD	1'20.066■14	1'20.333 13	3.401
24	26	O.GROUILLARD	FRA	LIGIER FORD	1'21.882 8	1'20.073■ 7	3.408
25	15	M.GUGELMIN	BRA	LEYTON HOUSE MARCH JUDD	1'20.191■ 9	1'20.260 6	3.526
26	25	R.ARNOUX	FRA	LIGIER FORD	1'20.872 13	1'20.391■ 2	3.726
27	3	J.PALMER	GBR	TYRRELL FORD	1'20.428■18	1'20.451 9	3.763
28	24	L.SALA	SPA	SCM MINARDI FORD	1'20.633■ 3	1'20.866 5	3.968
29	39	B.GACHOT	BEL	RIAL FORD	1'22.267■ 7	1'24.913 3	5.602
30	38	P.RAPHANEL	FRA	RIAL FORD	1'22.305■ 9	1'22.391 6	5.640

Thanks to the Olivetti engineers, the ratings for each Grand Prix event can be obtained in real time. Special programs permit making year-end comparisons on the basis of the year's accumulated data to obtain very in-depth evaluations of drivers and cars that far exceed the ordinary classification information.

Even children are strongly attracted by the Ferrari. Fortunately, these racing events seem to have been spared the kind of crowd violence seen at other outdoor sporting events.

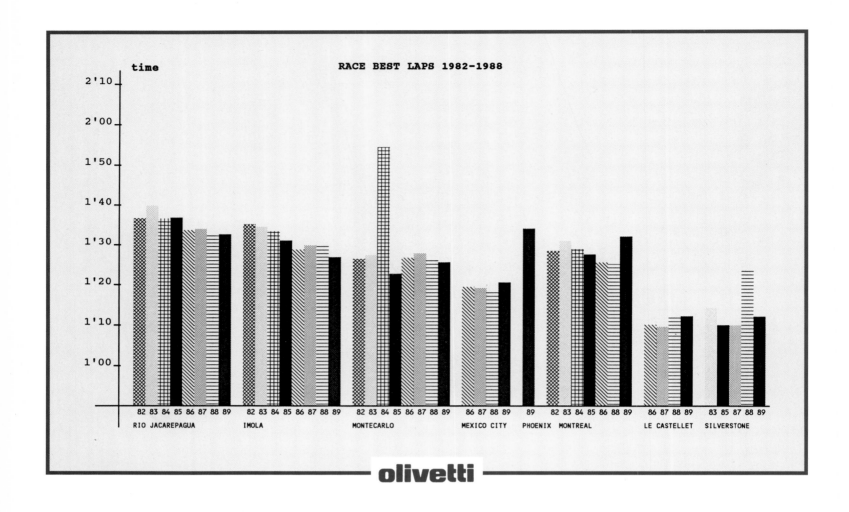

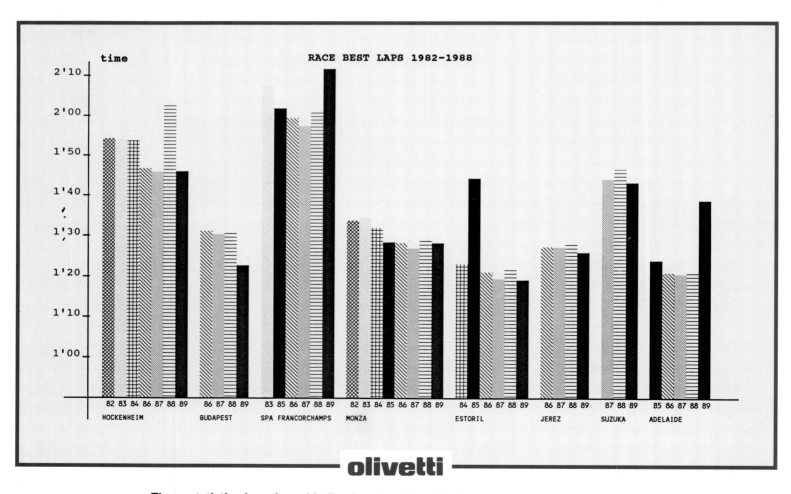

These statistics have been kindly given by Olivetti's "Servizio Computer per lo Sport"

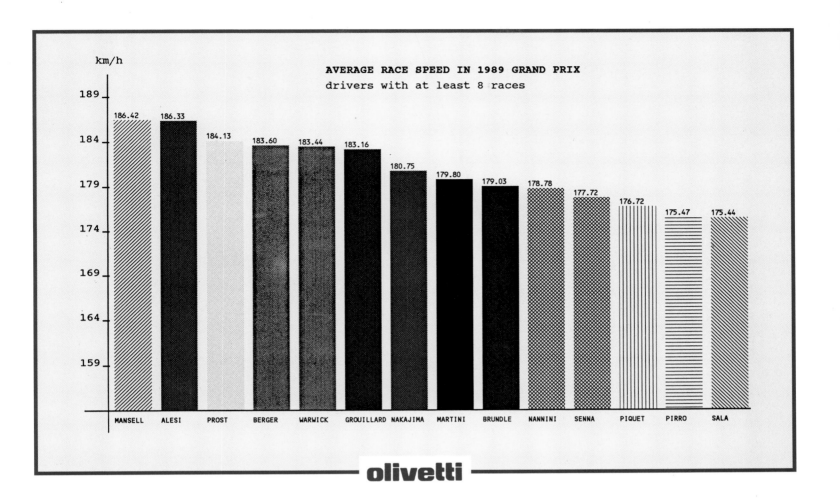

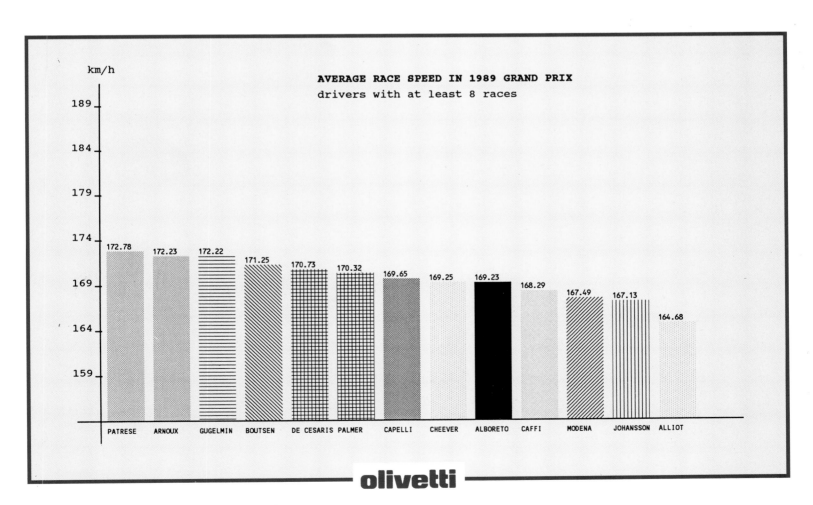

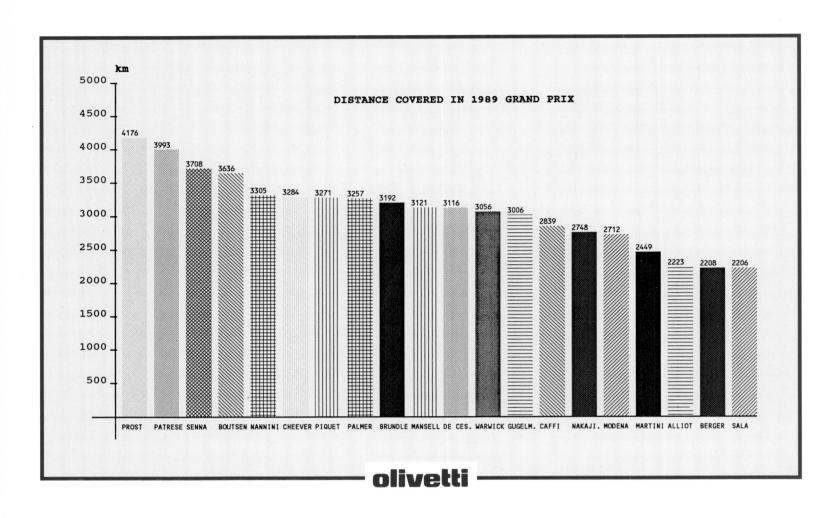

DISTANCE COVERED IN 1989 GRAND PRIX

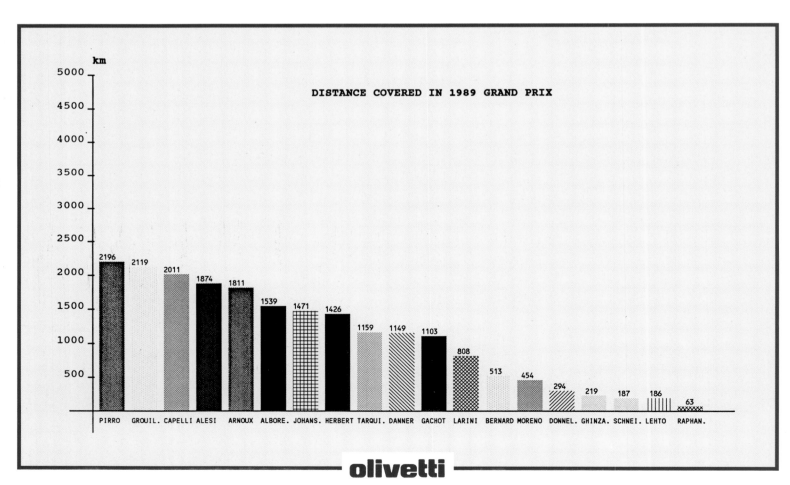

DISTANCE COVERED IN 1989 GRAND PRIX

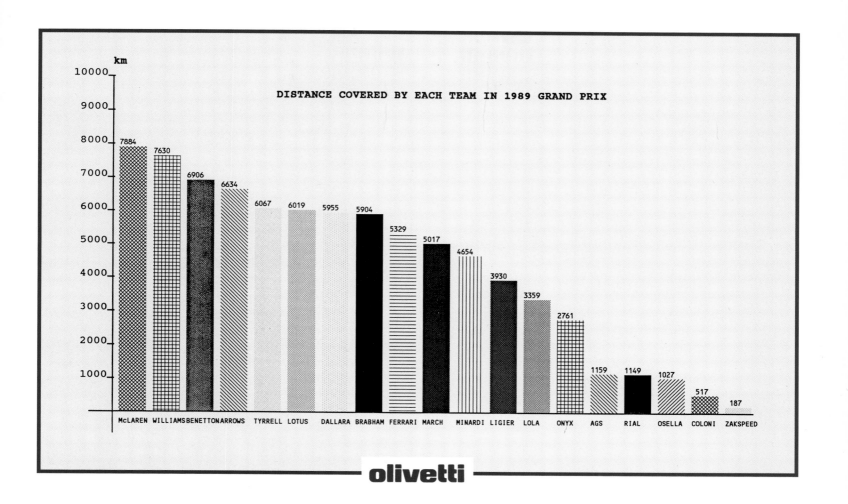

DISTANCE COVERED BY EACH TEAM IN 1989 GRAND PRIX

Team	km
McLAREN	7884
WILLIAMS	7630
BENETTON	6906
ARROWS	6634
TYRRELL	6067
LOTUS	6019
DALLARA	5955
BRABHAM	5904
FERRARI	5329
MARCH	5017
MINARDI	4654
LIGIER	3930
LOLA	3359
ONYX	2761
AGS	1159
RIAL	1149
OSELLA	1027
COLONI	517
ZAKSPEED	187

olivetti

LAPS AND DISTANCES COVERED IN THE FIRST SIX POSITIONS IN 1989 GRAND PRIX BY EACH TEAM

TEAM	FIRST POSITION			SECOND POSITION			THIRD POSITION		
	LAPS	km	RATE%	LAPS	km	RATE%	LAPS	km	RATE%
McLAREN	745	3515.070	44.59	499	2415.949	30.64	160	717.029	9.09
WILLIAMS	160	656.583	8.61	128	533.617	6.99	249	1036.591	13.59
FERRARI	127	570.007	10.70	295	1359.995	25.52	311	1633.424	30.65
ARROWS	4	17.560	0.26	16	70.240	1.06	47	197.956	2.98
BENETTON	2	11.718	0.17	82	321.048	4.65	79	387.790	5.62
MINARDI	1	4.350	0.09	6	24.960	0.54	2	8.700	0.19
DALLARA	-	-	-	6	22.788	0.38	13	52.252	0.88
TYRRELL	-	-	-	4	15.252	0.25	30	130.198	2.15
MARCH	-	-	-	3	11.439	0.23	32	143.940	2.87
BRABHAM	-	-	-	-	-	-	50	166.400	2.82
LOTUS	-	-	-	-	-	-	32	152.960	2.54
ONYX	-	-	-	-	-	-	20	87.000	3.15
OSELLA	-	-	-	-	-	-	9	39.510	3.85
LOLA	-	-	-	-	-	-	3	13.170	0.39

TEAM	FOURTH POSITION			FIFTH POSITION			SIXTH POSITION		
	LAPS	km	RATE%	LAPS	km	RATE%	LAPS	km	RATE%
McLAREN	101	459.658	5.83	70	300.063	3.81	11	48.427	0.61
WILLIAMS	228	1189.114	15.59	221	1120.920	14.69	198	992.462	13.01
FERRARI	142	683.444	12.83	77	356.902	6.70	12	52.466	0.98
ARROWS	41	166.441	2.51	85	392.254	5.91	102	555.524	8.37
BENETTON	174	850.277	12.31	148	745.807	10.80	113	571.977	8.28
MINARDI	10	42.930	0.92	69	299.100	6.43	78	322.294	6.92
DALLARA	73	282.308	4.74	79	302.346	5.08	57	214.144	3.60
TYRRELL	90	364.527	6.01	54	212.417	3.50	74	324.925	5.36
MARCH	36	167.718	3.34	53	248.234	4.95	35	148.696	2.96
BRABHAM	49	174.822	2.96	27	93.146	1.58	65	268.202	4.54
LOTUS	68	278.430	4.63	62	328.633	5.46	61	297.863	4.95
ONYX	3	13.050	0.47	36	140.391	5.09	16	63.462	2.30
OSELLA	6	26.340	2.56	5	21.950	2.14	13	59.670	5.81
LOLA	7	30.730	0.91	12	50.575	1.51	69	287.929	8.57
RIAL	5	18.990	1.65	8	30.384	2.64	10	38.572	3.36
LIGIER	-	-	-	9	38.356	0.98	71	295.534	7.52
AGS	-	-	-	11	36.608	3.16	37	157.489	13.59

POINTS CLASSIFICATION

9 points for each kilometer in 1st position
6 points for each kilometer in 2nd position
4 points for each kilometer in 3rd position
3 points for each kilometer in 4th position
2 points for each kilometer in 5th position
1 point for each kilometer in 6th position

#	Driver	Points
1	SENNA	26536.695
2	PROST	24490.273
3	MANSELL	13225.364
4	PATRESE	12625.130
5	BERGER	9414.967
6	BOUTSEN	7433.826
7	NANNINI	6534.332
8	WARWICK	2049.981
9	PIQUET	1820.139
10	CAFFI	1260.702
11	MARTINI	1229.974
12	CHEEVER	1160.678
13	ALESI	1140.342
14	PIRRO	1058.984
15	ALBORETO	995.411
16	GUGELMIN	980.615
17	MODENA	866.780
18	CAPELLI	812.097
19	BRUNDLE	777.780
20	DE CESARIS	750.794
21	JOHANSSON	670.815
22	HERBERT	604.017
23	NAKAJIMA	582.120
24	ALLIOT	511.071
25	LARINI	340.630
26	PALMER	319.891
27	ARNOUX	250.230
28	TARQUINI	230.705
29	DANNER	156.310
30	GROUILLARD	122.016
31	LEHTO	49.140
32	SALA	43.020
33	BERNARD	22.878

olivetti

The McLaren "family" portrait was taken to commemorate Alain Prost's winning of the 1989 championship.
Thanks to Senna's conspicuous absence, Alain was able to take his well-deserved center stage position without
any heckling from the wings.